D0717639

XS GREEN

For Emile, Mason and Avery,
getting bigger

First published in the United Kingdom in 2007 by Thames & Hudson Ltd,
181A High Holborn, London WC1V 7QX

British Library Cataloguing-in-Publication Data
A catalogue record for this book is available from the British Library

ISBN-13: 978-0-500-34230-5
ISBN-10: 0-500-34230-X

Designed by Grade Design Consultants
Printed and bound in China by C & C Offset Printing Co Ltd

Phyllis Richardson

XS Green:
Big Ideas,
Small Buildings

Thames & Hudson

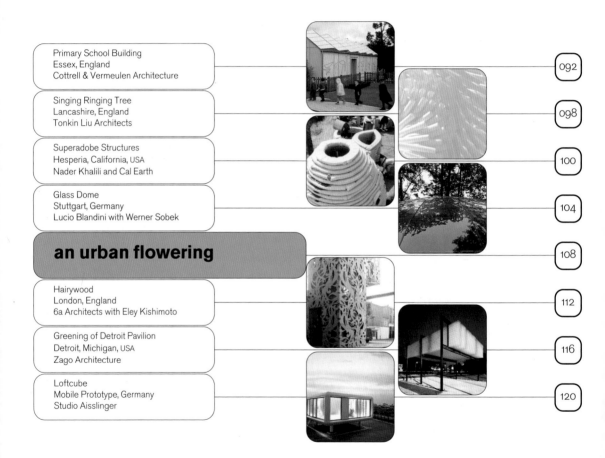

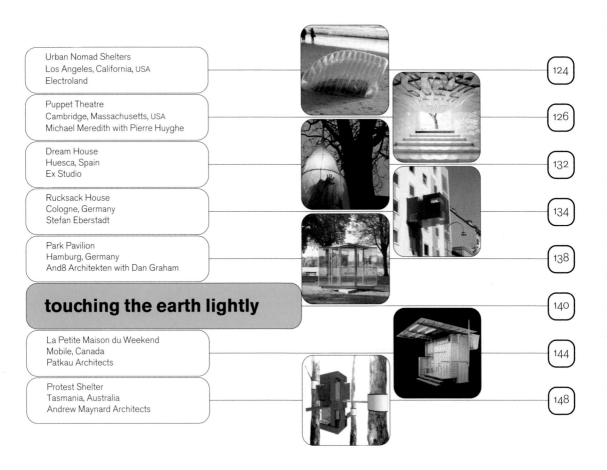

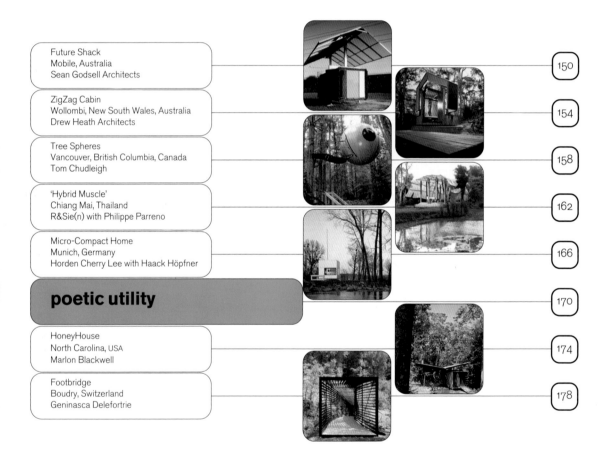

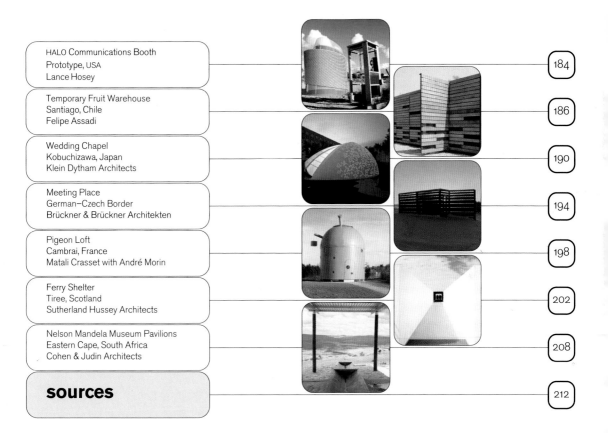

sources

Introduction

'think globally, act locally'*

(or 'think big, start small')

What does it mean to be green? While the premise of
XS Green was always about building that is kind to the
natural world, it was never meant to be exclusive. If we
are to grow the movement to save the earth, we need to
be a broad church, one that welcomes new ideas. *XS*,
both in its first incarnation and in its green guise, was
inspired by the possibilities of divergent thinking, by
the way that a small project can take the weight of
inventiveness much better in many respects than a
megastructure. We've all been drawn to the tactility,
accessibility and out-and-out cuteness of small
structures, but we've also seen how something used in
a limited space can have much larger repercussions.
Nowhere is this more important than in the fight to
preserve and to repair our natural environment.

This urgency cries out for all comers; idea
merchants, no matter what their chosen form, need to
be recognized and encouraged. In assembling the best
works for *XS Green*, we looked at projects that were
energy efficient, that were constructed using materials
with low embodied energy or were recycled. We
wanted projects that were not only about building
well, but about seeing well, observing the natural world
through a particularly well-focused aperture; those that

drew us in and then threw the world open, or refined
our vision to appreciate what is right in front of us.

Seeing the earth well also means seeing ourselves
better. In this, we felt that 'green' extended to a
humanitarian theme. Buildings that help take care
of people, temporary shelters or low-cost building
alternatives, often go hand-in-hand with buildings
that are ecologically friendly. If we think about it,
we have to conclude that the biggest, most expensive
buildings are not usually the most humane. So
buildings that look after people can also be the ones
that look after the earth.

There are many views of what it means to be green and, thankfully, many proposed solutions. It is a problem of huge import to our generation, but if the projects in this little book are anything to go by, it is not a challenge that has stumped our more innovative minds. Certainly architects of larger projects have been grappling with environmental issues for some time. Norman Foster's Commerzbank in Frankfurt am Main, often described as the world's first ecological high-rise, was designed with hanging gardens and a vast central atrium that aids natural ventilation, something not usually associated with soaring office blocks. Other projects like HOK's Federal Reserve building, in Minneapolis, demonstrate how investment in energy-efficient materials, such as triple-glazed windows with argon gas cavities, can produce reductions in energy consumption. Technology aimed at addressing environmental impact is also advancing, with IT programmes being developed that can analyze a building's energy needs as early on as the design phase.

That hope rests on the will of many and the ingenuity, perhaps even the brilliance, of a few. In design terms, at least, there appears to be no shortage of inspiration, no paucity of determination or methodology. What is needed in ensuing stages is the will. Perhaps by noting some of the more exciting possibilities available, we can go some way toward inspiring that will, even if we start small.

The book is organized into five sections that, while not strictly categorizing the projects, provide a point of focus for examining their particular strengths and achievements. We start here at the beginning; the first chapter, 'The View from Outside', is devoted to garden follies and 'outdoor rooms', the kinds of structures that first led us to discover the appeal and distinction of small buildings. These follow the long tradition of nature huts or shelters in the landscape. Whether they are ornamental follies or variations on the primitive hut, the gazebos, garden sheds, tea houses and temples

In these pages is a wide and varied spectrum of approaches to building in a way that both minimizes damage to and supports our natural environment. Some demonstrate more obvious alternatives than others. All represent ways of designing, building and viewing the world that enhance our knowledge and understanding. Such a diverse display of ingenuity as represented here, not to mention the many that we didn't have room to include, represents an imaginative capability that must surely portend hope for the future.

are all structures used by architects to experiment and review. As places of contemplation, some for looking inward and others focusing out, they make a good beginning for our search for green ideas.

The second chapter represents both a bit of fun and a serious look at what kinds of things architects and designers are working with in their quest to improve and expand the notions of what makes a good building. 'Material Concerns', subtitled 'experiments with fabric and finishes', looks at a remarkable variety of materials,

from bent twigs to recycled washing machines, compressed Irish turf to cardboard. The degree of detailing and craftsmanship employed in these projects surpasses expectations of what terms like 'natural', 'recycled' or 'sustainable' usually conjure, even in the minds of the most determined environmentalists.

Chapter 3 addresses the subject of urban amenities and beautification. If we have to put something in our already crowded cities, then it should somehow warrant the insertion. Projects that make better, more intelligent use of tiny spaces, those that highlight the small amount of green space that has managed to evade the march of concrete, and those that bring their own element of wonder and beauty to the cityscape are all welcome here.

'Touching the Earth Lightly' is a theme we covered in the first volume of *XS* and indeed one that helped to inspire the book you have here. Architects who recognize by their very trade that new building will happen, look for ways to minimize its impact on the environment, while also creating interesting, influential programmes for the development of new practices. Making habitation that is lightweight, portable and self-sufficient is a challenge embraced by

a number of builders and designers, and we applaud their progress in its wonderfully varying permutations.

Lastly, we look at the beauty of utility. Architecture is often about meeting a brief in an unusual or unexpected way. When that brief is a small, necessary object, the challenge can be perhaps more daunting than with a larger commission, where there is more room for amenities and auxiliary pleasantries. Small buildings that carry out their primary functions, while at the same time approaching works of art, are like little jewels to be turned over and admired.

Breaking down the chapters in this way does not really do justice to the aims and achievements of each project. Despite sharing a common theme of 'smallness' and some degree of 'greenness', they differ hugely in geographic, philosophical and social aspects, not to mention the geometric, material and spatial contrasts.

And the difference is inspiring to behold. In a world where bland repetition makes for a lot of building in town, country, and in between, it is refreshing to note little points of anomaly. This is how we know creativity still exists, and creativity is what we need for the biggest challenge facing the planet today.

In the effort to reduce greenhouse gases and the consumption of natural resources, almost none of the projects here is an end in itself. Rather, each suggests inroads in a journey to a host of answers for our current environmental needs in terms of building practice that is humane, sustainable, efficient, wise and beautiful.

the view from outside

Follies, gazebos, windows on the world

In the past, these structures were meant to be visual delights, tinged with or wholly ruled by fantasy, bestowed by clever anachronism with the charm of age, the hazy appeal of an enchantment. They were mini-palaces of escape for the wealthy, located on vast estates, summerhouses to shade an aristocratic picnic lunch, a shelter for an elaborate garden party. Tea houses served a similar function, but for a highly refined, orchestrated ceremony. Garden temples were not so much for worship as for the mimicry of worship, playing at penitence. They may have been inspired by the primitive hut, but increasingly such follies carried expectations of retreat, of the woodland sanctuary surrounded by greenery. Was this an escape to nature, or from it?

If the primitive hut originated with man's effort to shield himself from nature, then the garden pavilion represents the desire to go back into the landscape, albeit in some comfort. The pavilion brings us outside, but also focuses our attention outward, since from inside – at least in these 21st-century versions – the focus is outward. The point is to place ourselves out of doors, positioned as sheltered observers. Are we only observers? Can we do anything to enhance the land we occupy, or are we doomed to mar the view by our very presence? These are questions that the green garden hut addresses. For some, camouflaging our intrusion is the answer, but for most of the projects included here, there is more to the pavilion than being well hidden.

These structures celebrate the man-made form in the natural context, as that form contributes to the appreciation of the outdoors. The buildings that do this most obviously are two modern versions of the ingenious centuries-old device, the camera obscura. In rediscovering the marvel that impressed the ancient Greeks, the architects from SHoP and Franz Berzl and Gustav Deutsch take us back to the wonder of seeing. The operation is simple: the darkened room has a small cut-out through which an image of the outside scape appears in dazzling colour and detail. Berzl and Deutsch have improved upon the idea by making their image a complete panorama of 360 degrees, whereas the SHoP team has used the most advanced digital processes to create a building of prefabricated components, thereby reducing waste of material and labour.

Mitnick Roddier Hicks' entry for the LANDed competition

(to create garden structures for the Philbrook Museum, in Tulsa) is also about seeing. Moving through the structure is like experiencing a giant box camera. 'Split/View' is about simplicity in the pure wood form, but is also about complexity in its array of angles and views, and because it urges questions about how we perform the basic act of observation. Another winner in the LANDed scheme was New York-based MADE, a practice very much concerned with craft and the physical act of building. Their work is about blending and reshaping the landscape gently, and bringing other influences to bear in a light-hearted manner, while giving nature primacy.

Nature is the focus of Philip Gumuchdjian's 'Think Tank', on a lake in Ireland, and of Contreras and Cortese's Mirador, projecting off a hillside in Chile. Juhani Pallasmaa's cubic gazebo, perched like a boulder on the edge of a glacier, signifies a certain tension between natural forces and man, whereas Paul Raff's slatted pavilion, Thomas Heatherwick's metallic 'sitooterie' and Eightyseven Architects' steel-shelled garden hut are all wonderfully sculptural shelters that demonstrate widely contrasting possibilities in material and form.

room with a view

Camera Obscura
Greenport, New York, USA 2005
SHoP Architects

A centuries-old concept – the viewing chamber – has been brought firmly into the new millennium by SHoP Architects (Sharples, Holden and Pasquarelli), of New York. Asked to build a camera obscura for Mitchell Park, at the northern tip of Long Island, the team responded with a design that takes their research into computer modelling to its logical and waste-saving conclusion – a building that is wholly designed and specified for fabrication digitally. Each part and fitting was produced according to specifications that were digitally derived, arriving on site as a 'kit of custom parts' that includes full instructions and is ready for assembly. This highly customized prefab approach created a building that is totally unique, takes advantage of the latest building and material technology, and yet is modestly priced.

The lower costs were the result of the streamlined efficiency that this process can produce. The architects were not using the computer design programmes just to create funny shapes; they took advantage of the calculation abilities to tailor their designs to available materials and fabrication technology, so that there is as little waste of material and labour as possible. The dimensions of a door or wall panel could be adapted to fit existing sizes of metal sheeting, for example; still larger than standard size (in the case of the door), but resulting in less waste and work in cutting it down.

This is not to say that the team's creative achievements were not a primary inspiration. The organic form of the building came out of blending the circular viewing-chamber shape with the rectangular entry, thus creating a smooth transition from outside

to the darkened interior. That dark room, onto which the outside view is projected, was clad in black Skatelite, a material normally used for skateboard- and extreme-sport parks because of its ability to take on a high degree of curvature. Here, it succeeds in darkening the room and serving as a robust, curved-wall cladding that will bear up well under constant public use. The oversized door was built on a vertical pivot, rather than hinges, for durability and ease of use. Covered in zinc panels, it adds to the tactile nature of the building. The image from outside is projected onto a circular table inside, which can be raised or lowered to adjust for focal depth, in much the same way as operating a camera.

exploded axonometric

[pages 20–21] The wavy shape of the camera obscura was the result of combining the circular chamber with the rectangular entry. From some angles, the building resembles a sea snail or other gastropod.
[previous pages] All the elements were digitally specified and arrived on site ready to assemble. The 'camera' rotates 360 degrees, and the image it casts inside is 1.8 metres across, taking in the elements of Mitchell Park, the marina and Shelter Island beyond.

exploded axonometric

[opposite] The oversized door opens on a pivot and is clad in zinc panels. Openings in the wood cladding, resembling fish gills, allow for ventilation.
[this page] Exploded axonometrics demonstrate the stages of assembly. The zinc-and-wood exterior blends with the building materials used around the bay.

drama unfolding

Garden Hut
Sant Miquel de Cruïlles, Spain 2004
Eightyseven Architects

It has all the quirky character of an ornamental folly, set in a large private garden amid fruit trees and immaculate green lawns. The swimming pool laps and splashes nearby. But this geometric puzzle of a building is far more practical than its fantastically decadent historical predecessors. As well as being a model of sustainability and environmental responsibility, it is also rather interesting to look at and to look out from.

Artur Carulla and Rita Lambert of Eightyseven Architects were asked to create a building that could be used as a storeroom in winter, and as a summer pool/garden pavilion. Combining sliding and folding doors and window openings with glazed skylights, they came up with something that easily transforms for use in all seasons. In detailing the construction, the pair then combined functionality with ecological acuity, choosing materials like wood for its low embodied energy, and Corten steel for its longevity and durability. The timber used to clad the interior surfaces was sourced from a certified sustainable forest.

To reduce transport costs, both monetary and environmental, and to contribute to the community, the project was designed with local tradesman in mind. The nearest village, which includes six houses and a church, is also home to an ironmonger and a carpenter, who carried out the work of prefabricating the metal shell and installing and finishing the woodwork.

In this area of northeast Spain, near Girona, the ruins of medieval farmhouses are mixed with many new, largely unimaginative developments. Proving that sustainability and support for the local economy are not always sacrificial acts, this garden-hut-cum-winter-store is a thing of sculptural beauty. Inside, light and shadow are cast in unusual shapes, while a view of the rolling landscape of forest and wheat fields beyond is framed by the open porch. The weathered steel recalls the solidity and patina of age-old structures. Requiring almost no maintenance, and placed where it will not interfere with any of the existing vegetation, this little building asks little of the environment, but gives an unexpected return.

[previous page] The unfolding nature of the garden hut is revealed: the angular, steel-clad box contains a welcoming wood-lined interior with the basic necessities for outdoor dining. [left] The hut was designed to complement a large garden with mature trees that could not be disturbed. The steel skin keeps the box watertight during winter, while a skylight lets in the natural light and the view in summer.

[left] Views of the surrounding mountains, hills and farmland from the garden perspective. Concerned with energy waste and the local economy, the clients and architects chose timber from a sustainable forest and steel for its longevity, and ensured the project could be constructed using village tradesmen.

The building has a 'fragmented geometry that encourages the visitor to walk around it, refusing to reveal its volume,' say the architects, 'offering a different view from every corner of the garden.'

going over the edge

Mirador
Zapallar, Chile 2002
Carolina Contreras and Tomás Cortese

Sufferers of vertigo might not enjoy dining in so precipitous a location; all others will appreciate this elegant Modernist insertion into the rugged natural terrain along the central coast of Chile. Springing from the slope of the canyon above low-lying vegetation, the structure seems to float with nothing to mediate its exposure mid-air – no tall trees, outcroppings or, indeed, competing buildings.

The *quincho*, local dialect for an outdoor room used for cooking and eating, was commissioned by clients whose house and swimming pool occupy the upper region of the hillside. Their objective was a shelter that took full advantage of the view of the Estero canyon and the river running down from the Andes mountains and into the Pacific Ocean beyond. Carolina Contreras and Tomás Cortese responded with a design that gives a delicate impression but is structurally robust, allowing people to 'move forward horizontally in a counter-slope direction', as if into a picture frame. It was this decision, the architects say, that was fundamental to the project.

To achieve both the structural rigidity required and harmony with the existing elements, the architects chose a minimal form and basic materials of wood, steel and concrete, leaving the building as open as possible. Pine poles made from single trees, some measuring 7.5 metres in length, anchor the cantilevered box to the hillside, which is reinforced by a concrete retaining wall. The poles themselves are buried 1.5 metres below ground. Steps lead down at

a neat angle from the semi-enclosed dining area toward another viewing platform. The repeating planes and angles give rhythm to the structure even as its geometry contrasts with the shape of the hillside. The building achieves the aim of being a 'room' that sits well in the natural environment, having the appearance of an observation post where the view is more important than the structure itself. As a habitable space, it offers a remarkable opportunity to feel both sheltered and free.

section

[above] The projecting structure
overlooks the valley and the river
running out to the Pacific Ocean.
[opposite] The dramatic topography
of the site inspired the boldness of
the design.
[previous pages] The concrete block
mirrors the scale and form of the
open dining/viewing platform.

Mirador

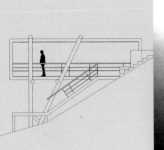

section

[right] The thick lodgepole pine supports, steel members and blocks of concrete contrast with the more delicate wooden slats and sheets of glass.
[opposite] At night, the suspended eyrie is a lantern on the hillside.

As a habitable space, this modern *quincho* offers a remarkable opportunity to feel both sheltered and free.

plan

light and hairy

Sitooterie
Essex, England 2003
Thomas Heatherwick Studio

The original model for this experiment in surface texture appeared in the pages of the first edition of *XS*, and remains a favourite amongst readers and editors alike. That building, made of over 5,000 oak staves inserted into a cubic centre, was seen by the owner of Barnard's Farm, a sculpture garden in England, who commissioned designer Thomas Heatherwick to create another version for permanent display. Given this opportunity, Heatherwick says, 'we thought, what if we take this a step further and make each stave a window?'

To that end, the team decided to make the structure out of aluminium, rather than wood, so that each stave became a hollow rectangular piece sealed with a translucent orange acrylic cap. Whereas the original wooden sitooterie consisted of staves all cut to the same length, in this version the staves have all been made to different lengths, and all point to the centre of the cube. So, says the designer, 'one light bulb in the centre lights them all; it's not fibre optic.' The cube is still at the core of the design, but it no longer dominates the structure; now the protruding rods really are the structure.

Getting to this point was no mean feet. While cutting thousands of oak staves to the same length was a formidable task, fabricating the cubic core with thousands of pre-drilled holes and individually machining 4,704 tubes required the assistance of a specialist aeronautical engineering company. Heatherwick, who enjoys the crossover of technologies and specialists, was more than up to the job of coordinating a variety of disciplines. In the end, it was the texture he was aiming for. With the first sitooterie, he says, 'we were looking at ways to create a surface that, instead of being hard, would have some life to it. It would move like a field of wheat, swaying and undulating across the surface.' Here in the English countryside, where it competes with the swaying of the trees, the hedges and even, far off in the distance, some wheat, the lighted form is like a beacon, albeit one that sits low and bushy in the landscape, inviting comparisons with hedges, hedgehogs, and other strangely tactile forms.

doors of perception

Split/View
Tulsa, Oklahoma, USA 2005
Mitnick Roddier Hicks

In 2005, the Philbrook Museum of Art sponsored the first in a series of competitions to create works for the renovated grounds of its Tulsa site. Architects from across North America were invited to submit ideas for a contemporary pavilion, and the winning designs were erected in the gardens, which were originally laid out in 1928 to designs by S. Herbert Hare, a student of Frederick Law Olmsted. Rather than presenting whimsical architectural flourishes in miniature, as with follies of old, the winning designs all represented a consciousness of the garden setting, whether as structures for viewing the natural environment or for blending in with it. San Francisco architectural firm Mitnick Roddier Hicks expanded the remit of the humble garden pavilion from something that might frame a pleasant scene to a viewing apparatus that recalls the mechanisms of telescopes, binoculars, cameras and microscopes.

The long, rectangular wooden structure is made up of two wedge-shaped staircases at either end, capped by an 'aperture', and a low platform running diagonally down the middle. Looking at it from outside, with the projecting stairs at each end and the open sides alternating with closely spaced slatted walls, you are reminded of the visual trickery of an M.C. Escher drawing, and almost expect the stairs to run back on themselves, or to lead to infinity. From within, the experience is like a journey of perception, as light and images appear through the openings, like walking through a giant box camera. Playing on the dynamics of geometry and perception, the architects say, the structure 'frames the schism between the way things appear to us visually and the way we know them to be intellectually.' So how you see is not always how you think you should be seeing. The 'split/view' has to do with the way the sightline through the interior is made to appear skewed by the angles (the crossing axes) of the framed apertures at either end.

Being unaware of the precise geometry of the design, the viewer is conscious of looking through the pavilion, rather than at it. As a tool for seeing, the architects feel, Split/View 'reconstructs the landscape through its own conflicted logic', but even as manipulated along those conflicting angles, the natural light and landscape are still the focus of the exercise.

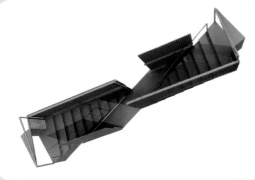

The distorted rectangular form of Mitnick Roddier Hicks' award-winning entry in the Philbrook LANDed competition is about 'geometry versus perception'. The structure, say the architects, 'acts as an icon for seeing, as well as an instrument for it.'

growing design

Vines Pavilion
Tulsa, Oklahoma, USA 2005
MADE

Ben Bischoff, Oliver Freundlich and Brian Papa founded their firm MADE as a 'design, construction and fabrication collective', and in their Civil War-era studio in Brooklyn, New York, they can as often be seen wielding saws and hammers as pencils or computer keyboards. Focused on the 'buildability' of their designs, they profess a close connection to the material feel of architecture, which comes across plainly in their winning entry for the LANDed competition at the Philbrook Museum of Art, in Tulsa. Perhaps because the construction elements – largely wood and rope – are so simple and so apparent, the two curving structures exude the playful quality of children's park furniture and the stuff of treehouses. The graceful positioning of the two forms, however, along an axis that runs from a gazebo to a garden path, and the references to the formal geometry of the garden itself, attest to the team's facility with more complex parameters.

The designers say their design 'borrows influences from Frederick Law Olmsted, modern aeroplane construction, timeless ship-rigging principles and simple backyard garden structures'. All of those influences are discernible in the elegant, sweeping tied-rope hollows that serve as shelters, benches and pergolas for the changing vegetation. From a distance, the two pavilions have the appearance of Native American woven baskets or dugout canoes. Then there is the springy, hammock-like sensation created by tensioned ropes strung between wooden supports. The shapes are all of these things, and yet extremely simple-seeming with components designed for easy on-site assembly. (The strawboard ribs, which support and are stabilized by the rope rigging, have been specified electronically to make them available to CNC milling contractors across the country).

The original gardens at Philbrook were laid out in 1928 by S. Herbert Hare, of Hare and Hare, who studied under Olmsted and was one of the first people in the United States to work toward a formal degree in Landscape Architecture. The recent renovation of those designs at Philbrook and the placement of the LANDed winning projects put landscape architecture on a satisfying continuum, but also demonstrated the great potential for modern methodology in shaping and preserving the natural environment.

At a low level, the ropes form springy bench seating that flows up into a pergola-style shelter. The abutting curves follow the geometry of the larger historic museum garden. Organic in form and material, the pavilion appears as a natural outcropping from afar.

'Based on the construction of an aeroplane wing,' the architects say, 'the structure is a series of strawboard ribs, perched lightly above the sloping ground plane.' The drawings attest to the human scale of the project.

panoramic projections

Camera Obscura
Aegina, Greece 2003
Franz Berzl with Gustav Deutsch

In an age when we are all giddy with the constant advances in technology, it is still remarkable to sit in a darkened room and observe the effects of such a primitive device as the camera obscura. Five centuries before Christ, the Chinese philosopher Mo-Ti noted how an inverted image appeared when light was allowed to pass through a tiny hole in a dark enclosure. In the 4th century BC, Aristotle recorded how he was able to view a partial eclipse of the sun using a similar method. Alhazen of Basra, an Arabian scholar of the 10th century, used a tent as a portable observation room, and Leonardo da Vinci detailed the camera obscura in his notebooks. From that period it was used by artists who traced the projected images for use in their work. Developments in this particular technology and the introduction of light-sensitive paper brought us the photographic camera. But how many of us have witnessed this very basic phenomenon of light first-hand?

Those numbers may be increasing with the construction of this illuminating little building on the island of Aegina, in Greece. Here, the Aegina Academy, a forum for art and science, together with European co-organizers, sponsored the exhibition 'Light, Image, Reality' to explore the form 'in which optical-acoustic media appear, and how they function against a background of global meaning and power.' Viennese film-maker Gustav Deutsch and architect Franz Berzl's construction takes the theme quite literally, using natural light to form images of the physical world outside. Their camera obscura is the first in the world

to produce a 360-degree panoramic image.

Set on a spit of land that projects into the Aegean, the building occupies a former gun base used by the German army during World War II. The cylindrical structure, made up of carved wood cladding on a steel frame, measures 7 metres in diameter.

With its low, solid appearance and small apertures, the building does recall some kind of heavily reinforced barracks or observation post, a fact that makes the inside-out effect of the interior even more intriguing. Perhaps it is appropriate that in peacetime here we can experience such breadth and clarity of vision.

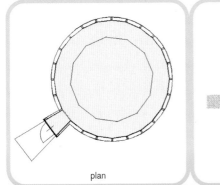

plan

section

Light enters through the twelve narrow windows to the darkened interior, to produce the 360-degree panoramic image. This appears upside down and reversed on transparent screens that are suspended from the ceiling.

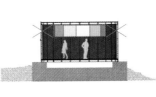

symphony in cedar

Garden Pavilion
Toronto, Ontario, Canada 2003
Paul Raff Studio with Sasquatch Designlab

It could be a stage for operatic events, or a camp shelter, the ceiling's gently bowed shaped recalling both acoustical engineering and the sweep of tented canvas. It is, in fact, a pavilion set in an urban garden, inspired, says architect Paul Raff, by both the centuries-old tradition of the Japanese tea house and 'common local construction techniques and materials'.

'I was also mindful of the architectural vernacular of garden elements such as fences and trellises, especially their permeability,' continues Raff. 'They sort of breathe.' It is the way the building sits subtly integrated with, and yet apart from, the natural environment that invites comparisons with the Japanese model. And it is the simple but highly functional design that reveals a home-grown, but by no means garden-variety, tendency. Raff and the team at Sasquatch Design went to great pains to determine the precise angle of the sun at the summer solstice so that the doubly curved bris-de-soleil (roof structure) would sit perpendicular to its path.

The roof, which opens wide at the front to allow musical performances to take place on the extended deck, is also tilted along the north–south axis to screen the sun at its strongest point. The latticework design allows filtered light to penetrate, so that even in cooler months this is still a sunny aspect from which to view the house and garden, and it does indeed breathe. The walls are built in two layers, with the interior layer tilting backward to make for comfortable backrests to the built-in benches. The two walls on the outer layer slant southwards with the tilt of the roof. Together the layers create a pleasant pattern of light and shadow, but also provide the necessary overall rigidity that eliminates the need for unsightly ties or cross-braces.

Such precision – each slat measures 5 by 10 centimetres and is set 10 centimetres apart – belies the natural harmony and appeal of the structure: the effortless blend of untreated cedar with the garden greenery, the rhythm of the lattice design (repeated endlessly in a mirrored tabletop), the criss-cross of shadows. The client, a teacher with an interest in music, wanted to make better use of her garden space. Now a path leads from the traditional 1930s house along the 38-metre rectangular plot to this shelter in the woods, a place for private reflection, outdoor dining, music recitals, a view from a different angle.

The owner of a house with a long, narrow garden added this modern wooden gazebo for musical performances and private reflection. The angles of the roof and walls were carefully calculated, so that the structure provides optimum shade in summer and natural light all year round.

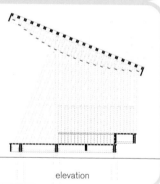

elevation

'My research had to do with ways architecture can enable better access to nature,' says Raff, 'especially the sky.'

angles of reflection

Gazebo Kuusi
Mäntyharju, Finland 2002
Juhani Pallasmaa

The gazebo as a quaint place in which to sip tea in the garden or set up a brass band in the park has given way to the structure as an opportunity for experimentation with form, material and spatial relationships. This version, designed by architect Juhani Pallasmaa for the grounds of a client's summer house in eastern Finland, first appeared as an exhibit at the Salmela Art Centre. Craned into place at the end of a winding woodland path on a rocky slope, it is a mark of civilization, but one that encourages engagement with the natural environment. It provides a flexible shelter in which family and friends can gather for meals and celebrations, or hide away for a bit of private meditation, always open to a view that recalls the dramatic landscape paintings of the 19th-century Finnish Romantic movement.

Glued wooden frames, stiffened with steel plates and cross-bracing, provide the basic structure, while the unusual vertical tilt combined with the generous window openings transform the building from one of rugged utilitarian design to an object of beauty and wonder. The inspiration and raison d'être for the gazebo structure was to absorb (rather than just observe) the setting of massive glacial rocks and pine forests, and the glimmering expanse of Lake Kallavesi below. With three 4-metre-high vertical panes of laminated glass on one wall, and three more spanning the length of the roof, landscape and sky are ever present. The 16.5-degree angle tilts up to bask in sunlight, but also, says Pallasmaa, 'creates a momentary uncertainty concerning the horizontality and verticality that alarms the senses and makes one intensely aware of the sky.' In this way, he feels, the gazebo is a camera obscura, 'altering our habit of perceiving the landscape as a horizontal panorama.'

Inside, a table with a small lamp and hot plate provide minimal home comforts. But the emphasis is on inspiring, rather than quieting the senses. Looking out, the feeling is of being suspended in an Alpine gondola, temporarily stalled on its journey toward or away from the mountain-top. So while horizontality is questioned, so is movement, and it seems possible to pause between motion and stillness, landscape and light.

Perched on a cliff of glacial rock, the building opens a glazed, upturned face and ceiling to the spectacular natural setting. Its blunted cubic form recalls a giant boulder that has come to rest precariously at the brow of a hill.

'The form of the building, resembling an erratic boulder, and the impression of flying were suggested by the powerful landscape.'

Gazebo Kuusi

on the riverbank

Think Tank
County Cork, Ireland 1998
Gumuchdjian Architects

However clichéd they have become, the words 'picturesque' and 'idyllic' are difficult to avoid when describing this riverside retreat in the west of Ireland. Architect Philip Gumuchdjian calls it the 'Think Tank', a reference to its use as a haven for contemplation, and also, perhaps, to its glazed, aquarium-like features. The day house was built as a quiet retreat for a client interested in boating, so the references to boathouse structures are not accidental. But Gumuchdjian was also thinking of chalets, 'a European perspective on Japanese pavilions', and even the humble cowshed, in his design for a building that seems to have peace written into the fabric.

That fabric, like the building, suggests both the integrity of history and the elegance of modern minimalism. The main structural elements are fairly traditional – wood, steel and glass – but their use and detail give away the contemporary design. Hardy Iroko wood forms the basic frame of the building, while silvery, weathering cedar is used on the roof, as decking, and for the slatted wall treatments. The slats offer some sense of 'enclosure and protection', says Gumuchdjian, next to the transparency of the large expanses of glass on three sides. This juxtaposition addresses the perennial dilemma of wanting to be in nature, but also desiring a degree of shelter and comfort. From inside the house, the feeling is one of floating freely. This is partly because of the way the structure projects into the water, with the pier extending even farther so that there is a dramatic sense of reaching, and partly due to the wide, open interior and generous ceiling height. The large, overhanging roof was allowed to dominate the building in reference to the local vernacular, and as a practical consideration because of the substantial annual rainfall.

In the well-worn tradition of forest follies, Gumuchdjian wished for the building to appear as 'a found structure, a simple and timeless object'. So the form and hierarchy of the architectural elements are almost iconic. But the setting, the reassuring solidity and the refinement of its aspects are more tangible than any imaginary idyll. This is a building very much in the world, as lovely as that may be.

The structure resembles boathouse, farm building and covered bridge – angles and volumes are carefully controlled to sit low on the horizon, but provide a generously sheltered interior volume. Wood, stone and glass correspond to the verdant hills, shoreline and water.

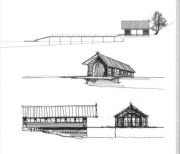

material
concerns

Experiments with fabric and finishes

When talking about environmentally friendly or energy-efficient buildings, people often look first to the visible structure, the fabric that makes up a building. Expectations usually run toward familiar natural resources, but wood, as we know, can be problematic unless it comes from a sustainable forest and hasn't had to travel halfway around the world to the building site. And while a steel-and-glass skyscraper may not look very efficient, the glass may be thermally advanced and the building may employ sophisticated energy-saving technology that allows it to control electricity requirements, retain heat or employ natural ventilation in ingenious but hidden ways.

Experiments with the material of building draw interest because of the visual impact and attractiveness of the tactile shell. Most of the projects in this book are interesting to look at, and most express an unusual character. This chapter, however, is about those that are really pushing the proverbial envelope. While we wouldn't suggest that the mere use of weird and woolly cladding demonstrates a valid experiment in green design, we would argue that experiment is good where it opens up the window a little more onto ways of saving materials, energy and ground space. So we begin with sculptural shelters that are created using dead wood, twigs and branches, methodically intertwined. In the broad sweep of a mass of branches is the intricacy of thousands of hours of hand labour. From this we move to that symbol of modern convenience, the washing machine, and the disused units that multiply in landfills all over the developed world. Here they are salvaged for the very watertight and modular properties that make them look like space capsules, but also make them work. And from space station to earth, the Turf House, made of bricks of Irish turf, brings the discussion of our dependence upon and need to preserve natural resources to the fore.

In that discussion is the concept of short-term versus long-term needs, and the possibility that all buildings need not be firmly tied to one spot. This idea is explored further in chapter 4, but here we present an inflatable material that makes fun, and useful designs from bridges to boats and tented spaces. Functional and fully collapsible, these structures make us question our perceived need for permanence, something that also comes up in a scheme constructed of reused wooden pallets. Almost indispensable in the age of storing and transporting goods and materials, these incredibly simple utilitarian objects are combined to form something enigmatic.

Such use of humble materials in constructing something that is both aesthetically pleasing and efficient is behind projects like the schoolroom built almost entirely from recycled cardboard, and the shelters made from earth-filled textile tubing. In both cases, the material has been recast in a durable and easy-to-use form. But some experiments will inevitably be at a stage where ease of use is not yet in the blueprint; rather, it is the achievement with the material itself that is remarkable. A tree-like sculpture was originally designed to be made from recycled scaffolding, but the size of the tubes would not produce the desired notes in high wind. Since the aim of this project was to celebrate the beauty of a windswept landscape, the architects compromised in their choice of material, but not in their paean to nature. Lastly, we present an experiment in seamless glass, an almost mystically transparent and reflective dome, not overtly green in its construction, but rather in its attempt at invisibility beneath the trees.

stick figures

Na Hale 'Eo Waiawi, Honolulu, Hawaii, USA 2003
Toad Hall, Santa Barbara, California, USA 2005
Patrick Dougherty

Anyone who made a hideout of gathered sticks and leaves as a child will appreciate Patrick Dougherty's fascination with twig-and-branch structures. A skilled carpenter as well as a sculptor, Dougherty credits a 'childhood spent wandering the forests of North Carolina' for his affinity for trees. It is an enthusiasm that has led to productivity, as Dougherty now has over 100 installations in the US, Europe and Asia to his name, with no two alike but all made of intertwined twigs. It sounds a bit primitive until you look at the various qualities of texture and movement that he achieves in the finished objects.

Invited by the Contemporary Art Museum in Honolulu to create an installation for their sculpture garden, Dougherty was taken by a sprawling monkey-pod tree that dominated the rear lawn. 'I thought it would make a great foil for a sapling structure,' he explains, 'which would be located underneath it and ultimately intertwine with its expansive branches.' The Hoomaluhia Botanical Garden provided strawberry guava for the outer shell of the sculptures, along with rose-apple saplings, to be used as structural supports for the twisting, towering shapes. The sculpture was titled, rather inauspiciously, 'Na Hale 'Eo Waiawi', or 'wild

dwelling built from strawberry guava'. The dramatic flattened canopy of the monkey-pod tree now shelters a series of hairy-looking huts. Their triangular forms twist upwards into the branches, blending with the living tree so that from a distance the huts look to be part of tree itself, creating the illusion of an enchanted little forest. You expect the elves to emerge any moment.

Fairytale creatures are also evoked in Dougherty's recreation of the storybook dwelling Toad Hall for the

Santa Barbara Botanic Garden. Inspired by the California missions built by Spanish Franciscan friars in the 18th century, Dougherty assimilated the squat, dome-topped forms of mission architecture into his own reinterpretation. This is an ambitious project that includes a tower, courtyard, tunnel and an 'erratic element', an unruly path, which took its cue from a twisted pine tree that grew nearby and was created to 'unsettle the architectural order' of the project. Closer inspection reveals just how carefully the order has been otherwise imposed. Arched doorways, circular windows and raised architraves are all clearly discernible, as is the contrasting direction of the branches, which give the appearance of thick brush strokes that create changes in colour, texture and motion. These details are a far cry from your basic childhood den in the woods, but not so far removed as to lose the innate sense of wonder that we get from being enveloped by trees.

[this page] Dougherty's installation for the grounds of the Contemporary Art Museum in Honolulu consists of two pairs of triangular forms, twisted upwards until they blend with the limbs of a monkey-pod tree. The constructions are approximately 9 metres high, and are made from thin saplings of strawberry guava. [opposite] Interior view of the dome created in the construction Toad Hall.

'One of the best challenges,' says the artist, 'was to remove the leaves from the strawberry guava.' The exhibition coordinator's elderly mother, a former dentist, 'sat patiently removing leaves, day after day'.

Dougherty modelled the installation 'Toad Hall' on local California mission architecture. The surface texture and appearance achieved with directional sweeps of twigs recalls rough stucco, or thick brush strokes. Located in the grounds of the Santa Barbara Botanic Garden, the project is part architecture, part vegetation.

out of the landfill

Miele Space Station/WasAutoMatiek
Rotterdam, The Netherlands 2003
2012 Architecten

'Much "refuse" in its original, unaltered state is usable, but pulverizing it into a low-grade, raw material leads to a loss of quality and unnecessary energy consumption.' So say the team at 2012 Architecten, who believe that reusing, rather than recycling, is the key to avoiding waste and to creating interesting structures that take full advantage of predesigned technology and materials. The architects are not only interested in ecological considerations; of more importance is the creative inspiration they find in working with found objects, and the history inherent in those objects that gives added value to the redesigned new product. This could certainly be said of the Miele Space Station, which was designed using mainly refrigerator parts.

In Rotterdam, 10,000 refrigerators are disposed of annually, each yielding a wealth of insulating panels that, along with discarded countertops, washing-machine doors and fire escapes, could be reassembled to provide twenty-two homes each year. As part of a recycling scheme, a washing-machine door would have to be disassembled, the glass recycled separately, and the metal and plastic elements broken down, all of which requires energy. But left as a whole, these doors make great watertight windows. To prove their point,

the architects built their own studio, combing the streets for 'usable materials to harvest'. They then moved on to the WasAutoMatiek bar, which was constructed using washing-machine fronts and a pizza oven with its back removed. The bar was then rebuilt as the Miele Space Station, an information centre/office from which the firm could work on their Recyclicity project, aimed at achieving more efficient reuse of materials within the construction industry.

The structure was named for Miele, the manufacturer of most of the reused parts. Glass elements from washing-machine doors are used for windows and a water basin, with the side panels forming walls and the drums becoming speaker stands. The insides of refrigerator doors were used for kitchen storage, and sails supplied tent space. This continual reinvention through reassembling of parts is a practice that the team at 2012 refers to as 'process architecture'.

Rather than pursuing a linear approach, which sees a building handed from one owner to another, they see their work as part of a 'continuous stream of creation and recreation'. There must be a certain acceptance of the ephemeral nature of construction in order to operate in this way. But given the amount of waste produced every year, particularly in the construction industry itself, this temporary state of affairs is already a reality, and one worth coming to grips with.

Named after the washing-machine manufacturer, the Miele Space Station makes new space from old appliances. Automobile tires, sail canvas and second-hand steel-and-acrylic panels were added to the washing-machine doors and refrigerator components to make a café/bar that was then turned into an office space.

of the earth

Turf House
Venice Biennale, Italy 2000
de Paor Architects

The Venice Biennale is always a showcase for the wild and woolly, and sometimes for the magical. In 2000, architect Tom de Paor captured a bit of Celtic mysticism with his construction Turf House, made of transported Irish soil. The turf comprised a gift from Ireland to the smaller island of Venice, as a gesture of solidarity and in celebration of Bloom's Day, June 16, 2000. The 21.12 tons of compressed peat was delivered in the form of 40,224 briquettes, strapped with polypropylene into 1,676 individually numbered bales. The bales were then assembled into a 'slumped-block' form. The calorific value of the donation was calculated to 373,782 megajoules, containing 2,534 tons of native Irish water and 63.9 kilograms of sulphur. The numbers mask the fact that this is a statement about the profundity of national identity, not so much with a governing entity, as with the physical land.

Stacked into their angled, corbel-walled block, the bales demarcate three inner chambers, two passages and one open courtyard. The three rooms are interpreted as a 'miniature labyrinth, or abstracted confessional'. Rather than being a mere exercise in quantification, the structure, or the material of its parts, is a physical and spiritual offering from one historic, largely Catholic, water-logged island to another. De Paor says his aim was 'to construct a sensory pavilion, an intelligent structure, a speculation on land and Santa's grotto'. Saints Nicholas of Myra, Lido, Manhattan and Dublin are all invoked by the architect, as are comparisons between the lagoon and the peat

bog as repositories of religious and cultural relics.

Apart from its metaphysical associations, the Turf House represents a physical connection to the land in the dependence on peat for fuel and heat, and in its structural properties, as made manifest here. Unlike man's relationship with trees, which he can replant and manage, there is no reciprocity in the use of turf – it cannot be replenished and a significant portion of the bogs of Ireland, according to de Paor, will be exhausted before the middle of this century. Bound up in the Irish legal system, which contains legislation and designated bodies governing the harvesting of the peat, and through the actual physical artefacts preserved in the bogs, a briquette of heat-sealed peat is a veritable piece of Ireland. Demolished by the Commune de Venezia Environmental Department on August 31, 2000, the pavilion lives on through its constituent parts – the turf briquettes were decompressed and spread out across the public gardens of the city.

[right] The thick walls are reminiscent of a fortress or tomb, both of which recall the history of the peat bogs.
[below right] A bench constructed of more peat briquettes offers a place for rest and information.

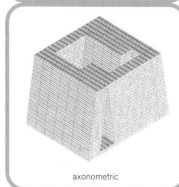

axonometric

material concerns

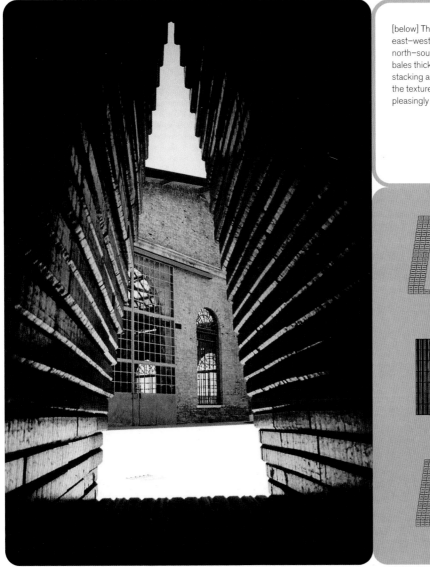

[below] The plan shows the stacked east–west walls and the corbelled north–south walls, which are three-bales thick. Despite such careful stacking and corbelling of the bales, the texture and imperfections are pleasingly apparent.

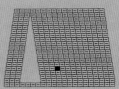

north elevation

plan

section

A rubber cast of a double bale of briquettes was made to hold information cards for passers-by. They also hint at the inherent value of the peat. 'Every day it becomes more urgent to consider the future of the vast tracts [of drained bogs],' says de Paor, 'and to give protection to the few remaining boglands.'

The aim, says the architect, was to construct 'a sensory pavilion, an intelligent structure, a speculation on land and Santa's grotto.'

The state of being and not being is what interests Lambert Kamps, the idea that a structure can exist when you need it and disappear when not in use. Also, he just seems to like inflating stuff. Perhaps it is this bulbous, stretched, bobbing nature of his creations that makes them seem like a lot more fun than most permanent buildings, bringing to mind the delights of funfairs and other outdoor festivals. But though they may look like fun houses for adults (and one of his inventions is just that), they are serious works of structural integrity and utility.

The Ferry Go Round, designed in collaboration with Tjeerd Veenhoven, is more of a boat than a building, but it exemplifies Kamps' principles of making structure where there was none, using it, and then putting it away. Should you need a ferry to cross the water in Groningen, for example, then you could have one – 7 metres square with a 3-metre-high protective roof – take it across the water, and then pack it away until you need it for the next crossing. Yes, we've had inflatable

rafts and dinghies for years now, but this is puffing up on a larger scale, for public service and a jolly time out. Made of 'fabric, aluminium, foam and a lot of other materials', the Ferry Go Round expresses its green credentials mainly in its portability and lack of any engine, which makes it both quiet and non-pollutant, though easily handled and durable.

Should you require a more fixed mode of water crossing, Kamps' Air Bridge can be blown up in fifteen minutes to span 15 metres safely and carry up to twelve people through its dimpled tunnel. Walking across it may cause you to be a little less surefooted than on more solid materials, but the beauty is in the bounce, and in the knowledge that you are walking over unbuilt space. Combining the buoyancy of the inflatable boat with the fixed direction of the tunnel bridge, the Air Bridge creates a comfortable walking space within its 3-by-3-metre interior, plenty of room for passing, or bobbing along hand-in-hand. The method is soft, flexible fabric covered in PVC.

Even in his more ground-oriented structures, Kamps is interested in movement. His Space Maker is an interactive tent structure with a ceiling that inflates as the user moves through the space. Sticking to his maxim that unused structure makes waste, he created the tent to be totally collapsible when not in use, but also partly collapsible when not completely occupied. The ceiling hangs at a low-lying 1.2 metres until a person approaches within, tripping a sensor that causes one of the many small blowers to emit hot air into the space. The tent ceiling rises to a comfortable 3 metres and continues billowing at that height until bodies move away from the space. Perhaps inspired by the playful behaviour of some of the participants upon entering the Space Maker and testing out the up-and-down motion of the ceiling, in 2004 Kamps created a festival tent, designed as part of a game he invented. This fun tent inflates in five minutes and is also used for presentations and festivals around Holland.

Kamps' experiments in inflatable architecture range from the Air Bridge [previous page and opposite] to the Ferry Go Round [above] to an interactive festival tent [following pages]. The ferry was constructed for the Noorderzon Festival in the Dutch city of Groningen. The bridge spans 15 metres, and can be inflated in a quarter of an hour and hold up to twelve people. Though, the architect warns, 'the more people on it, the more it bends'.

'I thought it would be handy if buildings did not exist when they were not used,' says the architect. 'Building with air was my solution.'

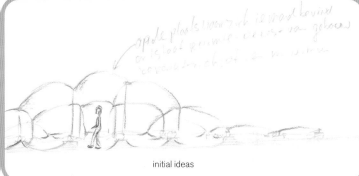

sketch plans

Kamps' Space Maker is inflated by a single machine to a height of approximately 1.5 metres. Smaller machines connected to sensors in the floor then cause sections to inflate higher as people move nearer. The tent is connected to the floor throughout by cables that become shorter or longer as the roof moves.

initial ideas

filling the void

Big Orbits
Buffalo, New York, USA 2001
Mehrdad Hadighi with Frank Fantauzzi

Inspiration often comes from unlikely sources. Asked to create a site-specific installation for a local art gallery, architect Mehrdad Hadighi and colleague Frank Fantauzzi scratched their chins and started asking questions. What was the building about? Tipped off by the unusual thickness of the walls (1 metre), they investigated further and found that it used to be storehouse for blocks of ice. They considered the gallery name, 'Big Orbits'. They looked around a town that has been a centre for industry for years and discovered a city of wood pallets. And then they went to work.

'Of course we were fascinated by the thought of the gallery being filled to the ceiling with a substance like ice (approximately 100 cubic metres),' say the architects, so the idea of filling it up with something else emerged. The pallets proved both plentiful and ecologically apt, since the team ended up using irregular panels that were slightly damaged and thus destined for 'the burn pile'. Allowing for the irregular pallets, Hadighi and Fantauzzi devised a system of stacking them that would produce a structure that was sound, as they intended to 'carve out' the centre. The room was filled to the top, as with so many blocks of ice, and the carefully defined shape, an 'orbital void'

removed from the centre, creating the first of two installations. The second consisted of the removed 'orbital solid', which was then displayed in the gallery courtyard. That solid was then acquired by the Griffis Sculpture Park for their permanent collection, where Hadighi says, 'it is now a haven for bees and for climbing children'.

This is a project that is delightful both in its seeming simplicity and in the way it manages to address a number of issues, in this case the history of the building, the current use and name of the space, and the desire of the two designers to create a twin-themed project that would signify their dual input. It also expresses that genius for embracing the obvious, using the ubiquitous wood pallets to create both solid and void, as this is what the inherent construction of these basic transport tools is all about. Then there is the idea of pallets orbiting the city, of ideas orbiting or filling up like blocks of ice, solid and singular, and then melting together.

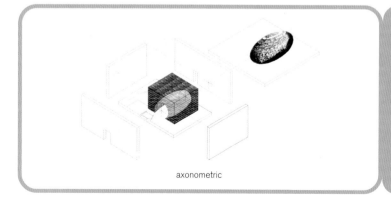

axonometric

To fill a gallery space and create a free-standing sculpture, architects Mehrdad Hadighi and Frank Fantauzzi gathered the plentiful material offered by wood pallets. The idea of solid and void became central to their project.

'I find collaborations to be one of the healthiest
ways of working. The process naturally makes one
question everything.'

cutting-edge cardboard

Primary School Building
Essex, England 2000
Cottrell & Vermeulen Architecture

Of all the public structures that architects might put their pencil to, school buildings offer the greatest argument for effective innovation, and yet must also count for some of the most banal and poorly wrought in Britain. From the Victorian exercises in imposing brick to ad-hoc Modernist boxes, it is a wonder that children emerge with any sense of beauty or enthusiasm. Bureaucrats and planners produce a plethora of excuses, most of them monetary, for educational facilities that basically amount to substandard architecture and building practice, which makes the emergence of a well-designed space all the more exhilarating to behold. This is a sentiment that greets the schoolroom by Cottrell & Vermeulen, a building that cost much less than your average build and was largely constructed of recycled cardboard.

Having already worked with the school on past projects, the architects were keen to explore the idea of using recycled materials. Looking at the structural possibilities of cardboard, they hit on 'the intrinsic strength of the folded structure' through studying origami. Carrying the folding theme through the design to the finished building, the dynamic graphics now covering the façade are elevation images and

instructions for an origami heron, screen-printed by artist Simon Patterson. The children collected card for recycling and participated in the design of the structure by taking part in a live BBC broadcast. The community engagement did not focus only on the televised events; the architects note that by being involved with the project, both the community and the children were exposed to the issue of sustainable construction and given a sense of shared ownership of the building.

Edged in composite timber, cardboard panels are loadbearing and insulating, and were manufactured off-site so that waste was reduced and immediately recycled. Cardboard-tube construction, famously used by Japanese architect Shigeru Ban to house earthquake victims, here performs both as structural columns and as palisade walls. The nature of cardboard, with its system of closed cells of air, means that it is inherently good at insulation. The project generated both interest and goodwill in suppliers, and donated materials and labour helped bring the project to fruition. Recycled products include Dalsouple rubber flooring, tetrapack board, polyurethane worktop and laminated cardboard sheet. The combination of winning design and varied methods of reuse and recycling has lessons for us all.

Involving the children in the building process 'not only exposed them to the issue of sustainable construction, but fostered a sense of ownership and pride in their environment that extends to the local community.'

Recycled cardboard tubes provide structural support for elements of varying strength and composition. The roof and walls act as rain screens with a breathable, waterproof membrane behind them. The project took two years, including one year of research and development, six months for constructing full-scale prototypes, and another six months of construction on site.

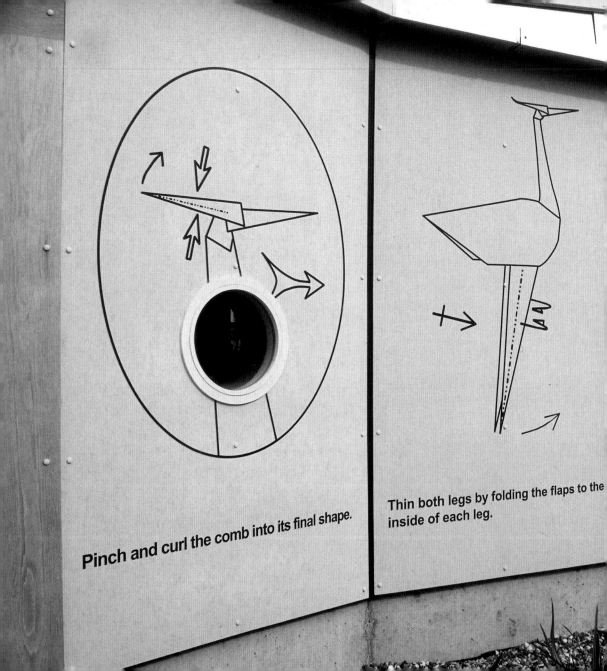

Pinch and curl the comb into its final shape.

Thin both legs by folding the flaps to the inside of each leg.

long section

card section

The new classroom measures approximately 90 square metres and is meant to be a flexible space. The 'folded' nature of the roof and walls adds dimension and interest to the open-plan room, while the cardboard pillars and visible fittings between the wall and roof make construction methods apparent.

sculpted by wind

Singing Ringing Tree
Lancashire, England 2006
Tonkin Liu Architects

It is a well-established fact that a remarkable piece of architecture can seriously enhance the cachet of a city. But the attraction is different in the countryside. When the Mid-Pennine Arts Council held a competition to create something that would entice people to enjoy the natural delights of East Lancashire, they were looking for structures in the order of follies, pavilions or outdoor sculpture. The idea is to create something that emphasizes the beauty of the surroundings, rather than focuses too much attention on the building itself. Such a work of anti-ego represents a challenge for a profession used to heroes who produce monumental works that often dominate a street or skyline. However Tonkin Liu, who won the competition for East Lancashire, have met the challenge of building for nature by reaching beyond the purely visual appeal of a structure, taking in the natural element (wind), and creating a work of aural architecture.

Setting out to design 'something that captured the essence of its place', the architects noted the very windy conditions of the site and decided 'to transform the wind into music'. But their design is more than a complicated wind-chime, or glorified version of pan-pipes. The Singing Ringing Tree is a work of astounding precision, made up of steel tubes, set in a spiralling formation, that are designed to catch the wind at a certain angle and produce specific notes. In this way, the architects say, they can control the chords that the wind will play. Their calculations are based on research into both the wind data for the four seasons in the area, and the Fibonacci numbering system, in which each number in a series is the sum of the two previous numbers, e.g., 0, 1, 1, 2, 3, 5, 8, 13). The pipes will then produce notes in that sequence: 1sts, 2nds, 3rds, 5ths, and so on.

By turning the whole assembly of pipes to face the wind, Tonkin Liu have created a dynamic form that, though made of hard steel, has the delicate appeal of plumage when viewed from a distance. Structural solidity is achieved by arranging groups of pipes in layers, with each layer rotated slightly to maintain the visual twist of the form. The architects initially aimed to use recycled scaffolding pipes, but the rough texture of second-hand pipes and their narrow diameter, which could not produce sound at lower wind speeds, convinced them to use galvanized steel instead. This concession, however, hardly mediates against the overall beauty, both harmonic and visual, of the piece.

sandbag solutions

Superadobe Structures
Hesperia, California, USA 1996
Nader Khalili and the California Institute
of Earth Art and Architecture

Sandbags and barbed wire are instruments of war that, according to Iranian-American architect Nader Khalili, can easily be turned into material for housing victims of natural and man-made disasters, as well as cheap alternatives to housing in general. Initially working with NASA to develop methods for lunar base construction, Khalili came up with a design that could utilize the crudest of materials to create efficient, solid shelters. He founded the California Institute of Earth Art and Architecture in 1986, which is 'dedicated to research and education of the public in environmentally oriented arts and architecture'. With a knowledge of native building techniques around the world, Khalili produced the structure he has become best known for, the sandbag, or 'superadobe', hut.

The building tools and materials are very basic, designed to make the erection of shelters in disaster areas easy for unskilled people with limited resources and almost no manufactured parts. Beginning with long, tubular sacks that could be provided by aid agencies, the builders make a mixture of earth stabilized with cement, lime or asphalt emulsion. If none of these is available, then a temporary shelter can still be made using only earth. The mixture is then poured into the tube by the bucket until the tube is full. Starting with the foundation trench, the tubes are then laid one upon the other, and held into place by layers of barbed wire, which, Khalili says, 'act as Velcro' to keep the tubes from slipping. Two basic line compasses are needed to construct the dome at an appropriate angle. Window openings are made using cut pieces of plastic piping, inserted between layers. Openings can also be made using arches. As Khalili maintains, 'the strongest structures in nature that work in tune with gravity, friction, minimum exposure and maximum compression are arches, domes and vault forms'.

Responding to the need to house large numbers of people in the wake of such natural disasters as earthquakes in Asia or hurricanes in the southern United States, or the war zones of Darfur, Khalili has posted instructions for building the superadobe emergency shelter for free use on the Cal Earth website. But the buildings can also be upgraded to the status of two- or three-bedroom homes. With plaster or other render applied to the exterior and interior, clean and white-washed living spaces reminiscent of Spanish and Mediterranean houses can be achieved.

[previous page] The construction method utilizes an earth mixture that is stabilized with cement, lime or asphalt emulsion.
[below] A tubular bag is pulled into place by a volunteer. The sacks are then laid out and secured on top of one another with barbed wire. The whole structure can also be plastered over, inside and out, using local techniques.

'To build simple and safe emergency structures, providing maximum safety with minimum environmental impact, we must choose natural materials, and, like nature itself, build with a minimum of materials to create maximum space, like a beehive or a seashell.'

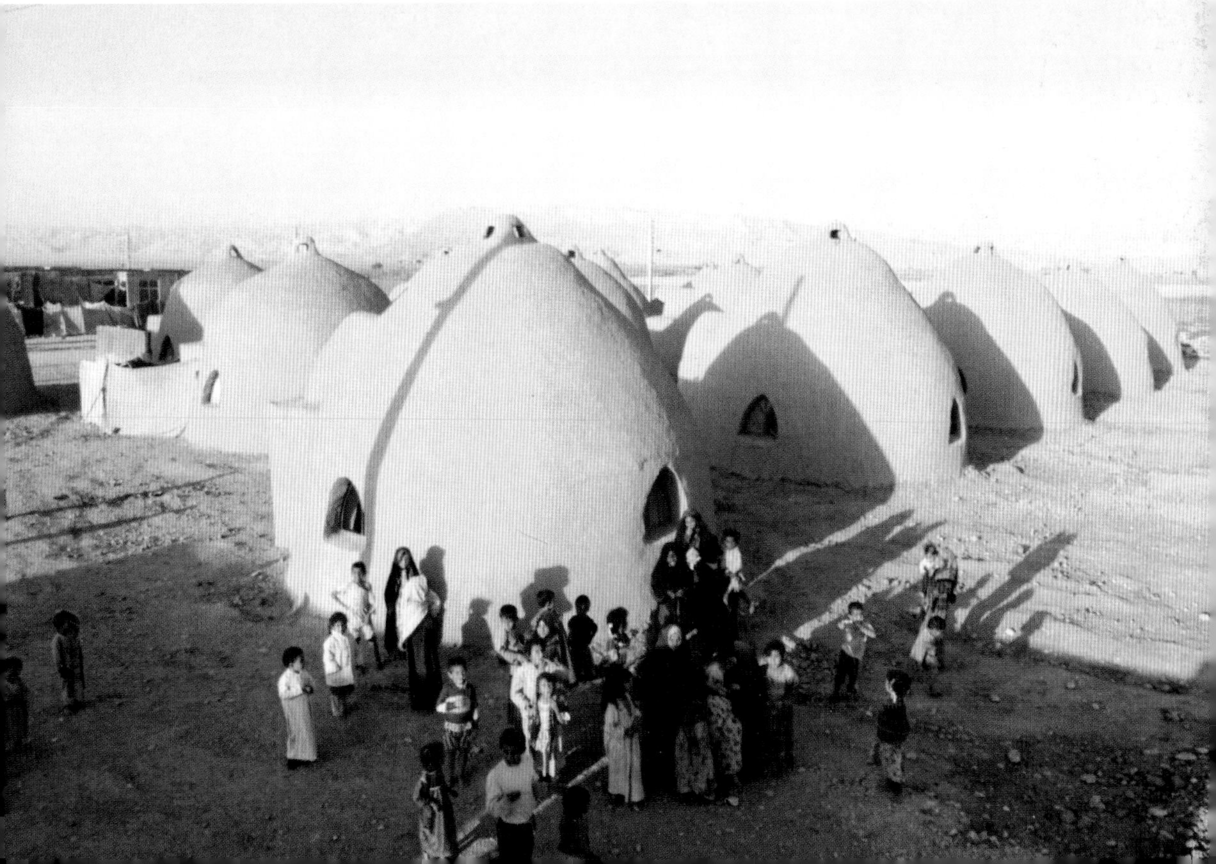

lighter than air

Glass Dome
Stuttgart, Germany 2004
Lucio Blandini with Werner Sobek

The aim here was never to make something small. In a place where revolutionary thinking is part of the syllabus, the idea was to create the largest frameless glass structure possible. The Institute for Lightweight Structures and Conceptual Design (ILEK) at the University of Stuttgart was founded by Frei Otto in 1964, and continues to attract students eager to experiment with new methods and materials. Italian doctoral candidate Lucio Blandini was no exception, and, together with his professor Werner Sobek, he developed this glass dome that seems to defy the laws of physics and gravity.

After three years of research, the pair finally achieved their vision of constructing a frameless structural glass shell that uses only adhesive to join the glass panes together, rather than any metal bolts or rods. Using forty-four pieces of curved glass, Blandini and Sobek made an almost fully transparent dome that is 2.5 metres tall at its centre and 8.5 metres long. Though they are only 10 millimetres thick, the glass panes are made up of two layers; one of 8-millimetre laminate, and one of toughened glass, such as that used in cars and aerospace engineering. Set in a dome shape to help take some of the load from the adhesives, the structure, says Blandini, has the appearance of a 'soap bubble floating'. Indeed, it does appear to hover, even with the visible titanium ring and stainless-steel supports that lift it slightly off the ground. Inside, the view is like being underwater as the glass distorts the light and shapes across the span of the dome.

Though they experimented with a number of adhesives before making their final choice, the pair are

still monitoring the structure to see how well and for how long this particular glue will actually hold through the seasons. In its first two years, at least, it showed no sign of weakening and the glass dome still floats in the forest of Stuttgart. Although the idea was to create something physically robust with structural potential, the effect of the prototype in the woods is something ethereal and deliquescent. Whether or not this formula for an all-glass structure will become a reliable and affordable building design in the future remains to be seen. For the moment, the idea that the physicality of structure might indeed 'dematerialize' and become secondary to site (and the woodland environment has a particular emphasis here) is something that might have a resounding effect on the way we might unmark the landscape.

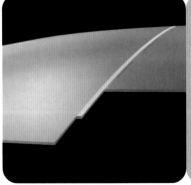

The forty-four curved pieces are composites of laminate and chemically toughened glass, held together using only a specially developed adhesive to create the world's first frameless structural glass dome – as much an experiment in glue as in glass.

'Depending on the direction and intensity of the light, the interaction with the surroundings changes dramatically. The shell can be a dematerialized envelope open to nature, as well as a reflecting screen that deforms shapes and colours.'

an urban flowering

Buildings that enhance the cityscape

As much as we might lament the growth of cities, they are an essential part of contemporary life and not something most of us would willingly do without. There is always room for improvement, however, even in small increments (perhaps especially in small increments). In this chapter, we celebrate buildings that enhance the urban experience through added green space, by aiding our appreciation of the green spaces we have managed to preserve, and through using the limited area in the densely packed conurbations in especially wise and interesting ways. If we accept the place of cities in our lives and culture, we know that our progress toward helping the environment depends largely on efforts to improve and regenerate the urban infrastructure that already exists, rather than abandoning unsuccessful development to start afresh. What follow are small gestures that confront much larger concerns within our built environment.

A project playfully named 'Hairywood' is both a reference to a familiar fairytale and a viewpoint from which to observe the goings-on at a crowded intersection in the city of London, an artfully enclosed window on the world that emphasizes solitude while it presents the urban rush. From London to Detroit, a city not immediately associated with an overabundance of trees, which is why its conservation-minded citizens became worried when they discovered that roughly half a million trees had disappeared in the short span of three decades up to 1980. An organization was duly founded to help replace the lost greenery, and a pavilion commissioned to serve as an outdoor classroom and exhibition space. It is a striking piece of urban architecture that is all about preserving the environment, but well aware of its urban context. That overstocked urban scene is what inspired German designer Werner Aisslinger to develop Loftcube, a stylish prefabricated dwelling that attaches to an existing rooftop. It's a solution to overcrowding in which the idealism of the 1960s and the efficiency of advanced technology coalesce. Aisslinger's compatriot Stefan Eberstadt has a similar approach, but finds spaces on the façades of existing apartment houses are ripe for exploitation in an effort to provide more space and avoid more building.

Nearly left behind in our forward march to increase both our living space and our green habitat are a number of people with more modest claims on the city, those who only require shelter in some form. It is to this problem that the partners at Electroland in the sprawling settlement of Los Angeles have addressed their Urban Nomad Shelters, basic provision given an artistic boost to help restore basic dignity. On to the highly dignified Le Corbusier, who left such an indelible mark on the development of modern architecture. To mark the 40th anniversary of the completion of his only North American project, a building for photographic exhibitions at Harvard University, architect Michael Meredith responded with a puppet-theatre venue that demonstrates the beauty of contrast. This is a theme that is taken up in a project by Barcelona architects, Ex Studio, whose answer to urban crowding is to create pods of isolation – small, womb-like spaces for introspection, hanging from a tree.

Lastly, we look at and through a glass pavilion that recalls many a glass pavilion but for its symbolic references to different religions and philosophical concerns, a collaboration between artist and architects that celebrates diversity, transparency, light and peace.

holiday in the city

Hairywood

Old Street, London, England 2005

6a Architects with Eley Kishimoto

At a traffic-heavy junction in London's East End, a small parcel of real estate squeezed between looming buildings was given over to exhibitions sponsored by the Architecture Foundation. For one year beginning in Summer 2005, this rather unlovely urban site was host to a series of installations. The first of these, by Tom Emerson and Stephanie MacDonald of 6a Architects, positioned a retreat from the grim concrete and gridlock, hovering like a lookout post, encapsulating the viewer, and turning attention away from itself toward the cityscape.

Collaborating with design firm Eley Kishimoto, the architects built a 6.3-metre-high plywood tower set on a raised deck that signals the entry to the interior courtyard, a public meeting place and café plaza. At the top of the tower, a small enclosed space provides 'an intimate escape for two', a pleasant sitting area with an outward focus on the urban scene beyond. The plywood has been laser-cut in an exuberant pattern created by Eley Kishimoto, and dubbed 'Rapunzel's Hair'. Inside the tower room, cushioned seats are covered in a bright landscape print, also developed by the fabric designers. While the shape of the tower adheres to the prevailing rectilinear forms of the surrounding brick and concrete construction, the organic, swirling patterns are quite playful and stand out in dynamic contrast. The 'hairy' design almost reaches out to connect with the nearby trees, lending the little room the clandestine appeal of a child's treehouse, or secreted observation point.

The architects were inspired to construct this 'juxtaposition of interior intimacy and public space' by Jacques Tati's *Les Vacances de Monsieur Hulot*. In the 1958 film, the heroine begins each day by opening her window and staring out to sea. To achieve the desired perspective, the director had a tower structure built to support a large bay window, from which the beach and sea could be filmed. Aiming to translate Tati's highly romantic idea (and the method behind it) to Old Street was an ambitious starting point. But the architects declared that their hope was to produce 'a new human interaction with the relentless traffic and urban environment'. In this they have succeeded, providing a place for solitude and reflection set well within the clamorous intrusions of the metropolis.

sections

elevation

panel detail

Laser-cut wood panels recall tower-bound Rapunzel, who famously let down her ample mane to her rescuer below. The window opens onto a busy street, set high enough to be a viewing platform, but just above interaction with the public space.

lovely as a tree

Greening of Detroit Pavilion
Detroit, Michigan, USA 2001
Zago Architecture

Within sight of a landmark of 1960s urban renewal – Mies van der Rohe's Lafayette Park complex – a new work of modern urbanism has been built. This one, however, is dedicated to renewing the landscape. The pavilion sits like a modular light box in the middle of a green space, surrounded by ageing housing projects and a busy thoroughfare in the southeast section of Detroit. The city, once known as the 'City of Trees', has long been associated with the less salubrious effects of the car industry – urban density, plant closures and decay – and, according to calculations by the Greening of Detroit, has lost an estimated 500,000 trees between 1950 and 1980 from disease and urban expansion. The organization celebrated their 15th anniversary year in 2004 by planting their 40,000th tree.

The success of the Greening of Detroit has also come through education and raising awareness. The best way to promote the use and care of green space is to bring people into it, which is what their pavilion is all about. In 2000, the group commissioned local architect Andrew Zago to design a shelter for sponsored events and children's workshops. His response was both a nod to the venerable Modernist heritage of Detroit, and a creative reinterpretation of the shelter provided by trees. The elegant, rectangular steel framework supports a stack of 576 clear, polycarbonate tubes, 9 metres long, that are arranged in rows of forty-eight tubes across and twelve tubes high. The tubes are not sitting on top of one another, however, but are suspended in wire fabric, leaving 13 millimetres between them. With the whole tilted slightly, rainwater must slide from one tube to the next, ultimately draining off at the lower end.

This openwork arrangement of plastic tubes is meant to act as 'a baffle for sunlight and rain'; light and water wash over and between the layers. In case the small amount of water that makes its way through the layers is too great, a space was left in the metal framework for a temporary canvas awning. This also allows the covered area to be enlarged to accommodate bigger groups. Metal and plastic are not standard choices for garden pavilions, but such pavilions do not usually have to function as urban architecture. This is a sophisticated structure that works to pull together disparate elements. Its east–west direction harmonizes with the main road, and the translucent glow provides a visual buffer between the built landscape and the park, like a beacon of environmental awareness.

This garden shelter for outdoor meetings and workshops works to join disparate elements of the cityscape. Its east-west orientation runs parallel to the main road, and the translucent glow provides a visual buffer between the high-density, low-rise buildings and a larger park beyond.

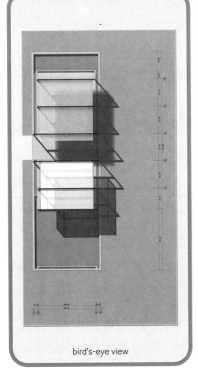

bird's-eye view

'Though simple in function and modest in cost, the pavilion has become a landmark. Its hovering, translucent volume – reminiscent of clouds and tree canopies – and its slender, poised frame belies its practicality, giving it the appearance of a work of sculpture.'

the high life

Loftcube
Mobile Prototype, Germany 2004
Studio Aisslinger

With urban housing demanding ever higher premiums, the question of how to accommodate more people in increasingly limited space is an enduring one. Vertical living has long been a part of city life for that very reason, but German architect and designer Werner Aisslinger has taken this concept to, dare we say, new heights. Aisslinger set himself and his team a two-pronged question. First they considered what 'a temporary, minimalistic domicile might look like that would suit people of a nomadic lifestyle, living for short periods of time in dense urban areas.' The second issue was raised by his immediate surroundings in Berlin, where the vast acreage of vacant rooftops suggested itself as the logical location for his new habitation. 'What would life be like on the rooftops of Berlin,' he wondered, and the Loftcube concept was born.

However, there were other inspirations. In developing his idea for a mobile living space and the potential for convivial rooftop communities, Aisslinger thought of the 'experimental hippie colonies' of the 1960s, like Drop City and the San Francisco movement that popularized Buckminster Fuller's geodesic dome. Social and spatial concerns converge in the Loftcube, where advanced systems and materials are used to reduce the space and energy needed to support a living environment, while also making good use of wasted real estate. Designed to plug in to the services of existing buildings, the Loftcube offers the luxury of a penthouse location with the affordability of highly compact, efficient design. Perched atop previously unused rooftops, the cubes do not add significantly to the urban sprawl and offer the possibility of social interaction, indeed a communal spirit, not possible in the confines of stacked apartment blocks.

The Loftcube's social and green credentials are less apparent at first sight than is the overall quality of design and versatility. The cubes require a crane or helicopter for placement, but once delivered can be built by two to three people in two to four days. Designed for easy dismantling and in compliance with international buildings standards, they can be relocated should the owner need to up-cube and move to another city. This versatility saves on the refitting that often goes with the purchase of a new flat. Although the overall dimensions are static (2.5 metres in height and an interior space of about 39 square metres), the variations in design are wide enough to suit personal tastes.

Degrees of transparency and natural light using glass windows and screens are changeable. The interior is articulated with specially designed Corian panels that act as room dividers and waterproof barriers for shower and kitchen units. Bathroom taps are mounted in the panels so that they are doubly functional, operating on each side of the divider. Though the Loftcubes might appear to be aimed at high-flying singles charmed by the glamour of rooftop living, Aisslinger is more interested in the communal ideal, viewing his scheme of small, mobile living spaces as 'less organized than Le Corbusier – more loosely structured, more transient, a sort of cosmic rooftop community.'

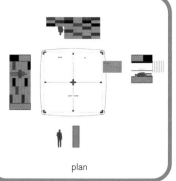

plan

The Loftcube offers a structure of basic parameters, with a choice of window treatments from transparent or translucent, to lamellae (slatted) louvres. A range of sliding and fixed partitioning panels help customize the interior. The dual-function Corian panels were specially developed by Aisslinger's Berlin studio.

'Think of small, mobile living spaces that compose a sort of skyscape, less organized than Le Corbusier – more loosely structured, more transient, a sort of cosmic rooftop community.'

nowhere to hide

Urban Nomad Shelters
Los Angeles, California, USA 2005
Electroland

It was a phrase coined to refer to the moneyed wanderers in the current age of budget airlines and global marketing, people who moved from city to city, sampling the finest and most unusual the world has to offer. But for Cameron McNall and Damon Seeley of the innovative design group Electroland, based in Los Angeles, the term has taken on a much less glamorous, but more humane meaning. For them, the real 'urban nomad' is the homeless person, and the shelter they have created is 'a humanitarian act and a social provocation'. The former refers to the function of the inflatable pod, cushioned on the bottom and protecting from the elements; the provocation they feel is in their intention to distribute thousands of the brightly coloured structures, to 'provoke a dialogue about the invisibility and marginalization of the homeless'. In the process, they have come up with something that is beguiling in its simplicity and logic.

McNall and Seeley maintain that the bright colour of the little pods on the pavement of your local street or underpass will succeed in highlighting the condition of the homeless; because the urban population has become so accustomed to seeing street people living under cardboard, they have indeed become virtually invisible to us. It is a harsh criticism of the demeanour of even the most socially aware individuals when confronted with the reality of homelessness. By providing something much more appealing than cardboard and blue tarp, the duo aims to remove the stigma of ugly temporary shelters from these people and associate them with bold new design. It is an elevating programme in that it bestows the dignity of thoughtful design, and promotes the assumption that these low-lying citizens are capable of aesthetic appreciation. There is also the idea that increased visibility will necessarily bring about more coherent plans for combating homelessness in the first place.

Though noble in their aims and frank in their observations of the way we treat our most vulnerable citizens, McNall and Seeley are not without humour. Their design is fun in shape, colour and texture. The vinyl dome with its toughened, nylon-reinforced mattress has been likened to a children's sleeping tent, a comparison that bothers the creators not at all. In fact, if children around the country were sleeping in them, that would only further Electroland's campaign to make shelters that are universally liked and welcomed, rather than condemned or ignored.

le corbusier revisited

Puppet Theatre
Cambridge, Massachusetts, USA 2002
Michael Meredith with Pierre Huyghe

The puppet-theatre structure is not what you would expect from an homage to Le Corbusier, except that it fits neatly under the Carpenter Center at Harvard University's campus in Cambridge, Massachusetts, the only building by Le Corbusier to have been built in North America. In honour of the 40th anniversary of the center, which is home to the university's Department of Visual and Environmental Studies, architect Michael Meredith worked with conceptual artist Pierre Huyghe to create this venue for puppet performances. The design started out as a 'pure box' that would be sited in the space below the existing building, which in Le Corbusian fashion is raised on columns with a sunken courtyard beneath. That pure shape, however, was then distorted through parametric modelling, and the resulting structure looks rather like it is trying to be stuffed under the much larger and heavier building above, though resisting admirably. Homage here does not necessarily mean subservience.

Up close, Meredith's construction is a riot of clever contrasts. Instead of the strict geometries of Le Corbusier's creation, here is a bulging and dented volume. Counter to the matte of plain concrete is the high gloss of white polycarbonate. Up against the continuous poured mass is an assemblage of more than 500 diamond-shaped panels, each unique. Rather than

having a hard, man-made impenetrable surface, the concatenated polycarbonate panels, which are 7.6 centimetres deep with raised edges, hold small patches of moss. So the whole organically shaped construction is like overgrown crazy paving, or an emerging swamp thing, as befitting the grotto-like position.

On the inside, to avoid the dark and gloomy experience of the tunnel-like position, the gleaming tiles bounce light all over the place, as do the coated foam benches that repeat the pattern of the tessellated wall and ceiling structure. As the entire structure is sheltered by the hovering building above, the panels, though bolted together, are not sealed. Through

numerous discernible gaps, light escapes during evening performances, illuminating the moss-covered shape and giving the illusion that the mossy parts float separately from one another. This was not just a nod to organic matter; the moss, according to Meredith, 'is a good insulation device acoustically and thermally'. He also notes that it was 'important to try to set up a collapsed relationship between the "organic" and the "technological".' This he clearly has done, producing a readable dialogue, a performance of parts, even before the show begins.

The architect created more than 500 interlocking panels to form a rigid structure. However, the appearance, aided by the moss-covered exterior, is of something softer than the rigid permanence of the concrete building above. When there is no performance, the view carries through to the building entrance.

'The theatre collapses the synthetic and the organic into a single structural surface.'

they're in the trees

Dream House
Huesca, Spain 2004
Ex Studio

A chrysalis dangling freely from a branch is one of those happenings in nature that is both common and awe-inspiring. Perhaps that is why the architects at Barcelona-based Ex Studio chose this form to encourage 'reflection on the relationship of human beings with their built and natural environment'. From another angle, the hanging form could also be perceived as some sort of alien pod, not found in nature, but out of the realm of science fiction or fantasy, from which some strange creature is likely to emerge. According to Patricia Meneses and Iván Juárez, it is definitely the natural world with which they wish to engage. There is this other surreal aura about the Dream House, however, which expands beyond the boundaries of man and nature to explore the infinite space of the human imagination.

With its delicate skin, translucent and pliable, it hardly seems capable of supporting a human body. But the Dream House is meant as a human refuge, 'an interior space for self-reflection' within the urban environment. That the chrysalis was designed as an urban treatment, and not merely as a retreat from the cityscape, makes its introspective quality even more extreme. Rather than taking us away from the urban experience, they want to place us within it. Though instead of offering us another take on the high-density built space (shoehorned into a Tokyo capsule hotel, for example), Ex Studio proposes that we cling to the trees, both preserving and using them for our own mental space. In fact, the architects have dubbed the project the 'urban refugee', making the user *of* the city, but not *in* it. Thus suspended – here using steel cables, polycarbonate and plastic – in womb-like comfort, we can take a good metaphorical look at ourselves and our surroundings. What are we likely to see between the limbs and leaves? That the natural and man-made world just became a more interesting place.

space in a box

Rucksack House
Cologne, Germany 2004
Stefan Eberstadt

It is a truth universally acknowledged that most urban dwellers pine for more space at one time or another. Stefan Eberstadt put his longing to good use, as inspiration for a totally new approach to urban living. The Rucksack House is a prefabricated extension, 2.5 by 3.6 by 2.5 metres, which gets its name from the way the cables that allow it to hang over the side of its host building simulate the shoulder straps of a rucksack. The idea, Eberstadt maintains, is a response to 'the claustrophobic living conditions I experienced in cities like London, New York and Chicago, small apartments with sometimes only one window to the outside world.' His epiphany came when he realized that instead of just looking out the window, he wanted to be able to step out of it into more living space. The solution he came up with, while radical, is quick and simple: a room that is craned into place and secured over the window opening of an existing apartment. Of course, the

structure has been rigorously engineered for stability: four spikes protruding from the open side are mounted into pre-drilled holes in the façade of the building, and the box is then suspended from steel cables that run over the roof of the building and are anchored onto the rear façade. This process only takes a few hours.

Eberstadt chose a cube design because of his own affinity for rectangular shapes, and because, he says, it is a form we trust, being 'logical, honest, solid and understandable'. The welded-steel structure is clad in plywood coated with resin, while the interior is birch-veneered plywood. Unlike his experience in small flats, Eberstadt created a light-filled space through numerous rectangular window openings, glazed in Perspex, that wrap around corners at the side and onto the roof. It is this element that gives the most freedom to the atmosphere inside the box, so rare in apartment dwellings. From the outside, the Rucksack House is

obviously suspended in space, seeming both precarious and unobtrusive. On the inside, with light travelling freely through the various window openings, the floating sensation is still palpable, especially as some of the apertures puncture the floor.

Though it is shape-specific, the rucksack addition does not have a designated use. That is something for the inhabitant to decide, whether it should be left empty for contemplation, as Eberstadt prefers, or equipped with furniture that folds out from the walls –

a low platform for lying on, a table or a stool. Electricity can be run into the cube from the host building. Eberstadt, who began his career as a sculptor, is more interested in challenging our perceptions of space and boundaries, in making something sculptural that brings art into public space, than in adhering to traditional building design. Believing that 'today, the task for art is to influence the design and aesthetic structures of our environment,' he will continue to look at space with a view to expanding possibilities.

[above] A system of fold-out furniture provides some essential amenities and simultaneously opens up more windows in the cube.
[opposite] The open side of the structure fits over an existing window opening, and is secured with four protruding spikes and cables anchored to the rear façade.

section

'Art cannot be seen as an isolated factor. Rather, it should challenge and interact with other fields like architecture and design.'

through a glass brightly

Park Pavilion
Hamburg, Germany 1999
And8 Architekten with Dan Graham

Glass pavilions do not garner much attention anymore. We have become somewhat inured to the wonders of transparency. But somehow this changes, as with our perception of many materials, when the scale is reduced to something roughly human in size. When New York artist Dan Graham, working with architects And8, was asked to create something for a public park in Hamburg, he had several factors to consider and potentially to compete with. Firstly, there was the precious greenery of the park itself, providing respite from the hard urbanscape. Secondly, the River Alster flowing majestically past, and, finally, the steel-and-glass office blocks that dominate so much of the city's visual impression.

The resulting pavilion is both sculptural and practical, fully realized and iconic. The glass, as in many a riverside setting, helps to refer and relate to the reflective surface of the body of water moving inexorably past. In combination with the steel framing, it also imitates the materials of the nearby office towers. But in taking those materials and focusing them down to a diminutive scale, the artist and architects made them suddenly human. The pavilion becomes an accessible and apprehendable object, something that can be owned by a single person for a moment.

Once inside, the visitor can appreciate the views of the surrounding park and trees, the movement of the river and the colour of the sky, while also experiencing

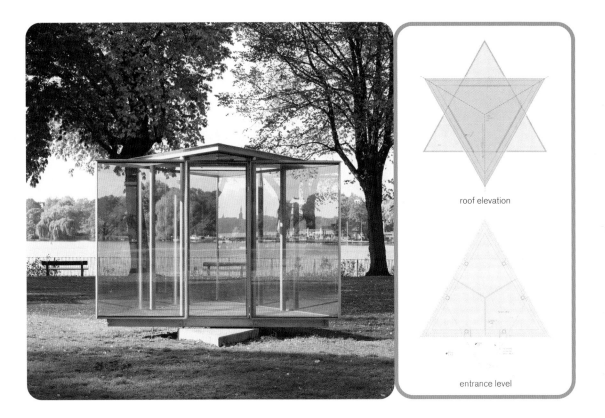

roof elevation

entrance level

enclosure. 'My pavilions are architecturally usable spaces,' says Graham, 'temporary outdoor shelters in an Arcadian tradition.' Here, the shelter is both arcadian and urbane.

There is symbolism, too, beyond the material references. The arrangement of two equilateral triangles, one imposed upon the other, alludes to both Judaism and Islam. Since light has great symbolic and metaphoric value in both faiths – indeed, in most of the world's known religions – the little chamber works as a sort of offering for the experience of peaceful contemplation, closed off to the noise of the world, and perhaps encouraging the hope of illumination.

touching the earth lightly

Lightweight, compact, portable

To touch the earth lightly was a desire expressed by Australian architect Glen Murcutt, citing Aboriginal philosophy. It is a theme that has resonance across the world. Since we as humans must inhabit the planet, we can only hope to minimize our negative impact. The first volume of *XS* brought to attention a number of lightweight designs, which were inspired by exploration into impermanence and mobility in architecture. Here, we again focus on those designs that are compact and adaptable, causing as little interruption to the landscape as possible. As with other chapters there is overlap here: Lambert Kamps' inflatable designs (chapter 2) are notable crossover, as are the Loftcube, the Rucksack House and the Urban Nomad Shelter (chapter 3). And a number of other structures included in the book are inherently less fixed or weighty than your average building, of whatever size. Making something significant within self-imposed spatial and even weight limits presents a challenge to designers and architects. Those presented here have taken up that challenge with gusto and with deft execution.

Weekend getaways are not the most green structures that an

environmentally conscious designer can put his or her mind to; by definition they represent an excess of money and materials. Vacationing is when many of us actually engage with nature, however, so these buildings present a good opportunity to highlight environmental concerns. Australian architect Drew Heath's ZigZag Cabin and Canadian firm Patkau Architects' La Petite Maison du Weekend are both ingenious organizations of interior spaces combined in compact entities, demonstrating craftsmanship and refinement of detail that would impress on any scale. Impressive, too, is Andrew Maynard's design for a tree-based protest shelter, a project that is thoroughly green in both structure and intent. Tom Chudleigh's Tree Spheres are also dependent on, as well as depending from, the noble arboreal giants.

Richard Horden, who has long been concerned with creating compact and transportable architecture (see *XS*, volume 1), has developed a new highly efficient and technologically advanced living unit in concert with Stuttgart-based architect Lydia Haack and their student designers. The Micro-Compact Home was conceived as an answer to the need for many units in a small space, as, for example, in university campuses, where people are willing and able to keep their demands for indoor space to a minimum. Horden's compact project – like students – demonstrates a genius for multi-tasking and looking remarkably poised at the same time.

Sean Godsell's reuse of shipping containers has taken a humanitarian approach. His idea was to assemble an all-in-one efficiency unit as emergency shelter in the ample storage space of the standard-sized containers, which are, obviously, highly transportable and thus ready for use all over the world where quick and easy housing is needed. It is not clear how such a structure would fare in the rice paddies of Chiang Mai, which is why French architects R&Sie(n) laid a concrete foundation for their multi-purpose artist's studio. The slab, however, is the only permanent piece in a building that is a living object, powered by animal strength and clad in a flexible transparent skin. Both the subject of and a character in a surreal film project by director Philippe Parreno, the building holds up the question of life imitating art and proposes that it is no bad thing.

compact charisma

La Petite Maison du Weekend
Mobile, Canada 1998–99
Patkau Architects

Even if your first home is a noble pile, the Petite Maison du Weekend is a luxurious offering, something like a quality leather overnight bag, beautiful and yet practical at the same time, with all the compartments you need to carry luxuries as well as necessities.

Here, the luxury is in the quality of materials, in the simple arrangement of spaces, and the ease with which it all comes together. The Petite Maison was designed by Patkau Architects for the 'Fabrications' exhibition held at the Wexner Center for the Arts in Columbus, Ohio, which featured full-scale installations that explored new ways in which to exhibit architecture within the museum. The firm's own explorations resulted in a totally self-sufficient shelter that would sit well next to river, lake or mountain, and would provide a high degree of comfort that required a petite amount of space and environmental disruption.

The construction marries simplicity with functionality. A steel base supports planes of hemlock and plywood that act as dividers, hold integrated shelving, and work as sliding partitions. The 26-square-metre structure includes a sleeping loft, open-and-closed kitchen area, composting toilet, shower and sheltered porch. Heat, warmth and light are all provided without the need for power lines or plug-ins to mains services. The oversized glass roof maintains a dry perimeter while collecting rainwater in a canvas reservoir, which is then distributed to the gravity shower and sink. Photovoltaic cells on the roof feed solar energy into a small battery bank that powers the mini high-performance refrigerator and low-voltage lights. A small propane burner is also provided in the kitchen area.

On a larger scale this would be a dream house, with all the details well thought out and beautifully designed. At this size, it is a small wonder with much larger implications for improving on standard housing models. All of the components were designed to be shop-manufactured and assembled on site in about a week, leaving plenty of days and evenings to admire one's handiwork, not to mention the view.

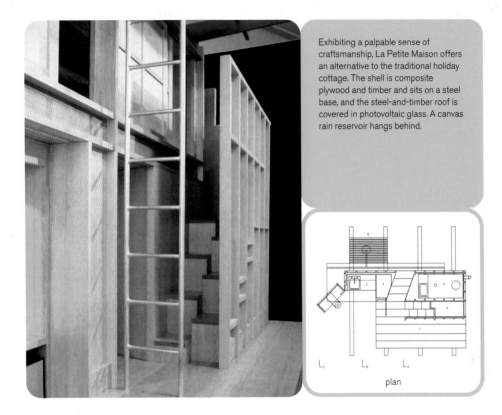

Exhibiting a palpable sense of craftsmanship, La Petite Maison offers an alternative to the traditional holiday cottage. The shell is composite plywood and timber and sits on a steel base, and the steel-and-timber roof is covered in photovoltaic glass. A canvas rain reservoir hangs behind.

plan

'La Petite Maison du Weekend generates its own electricity, collects and distributes rainwater, and composts waste using only the natural dynamics of the site.'

saving the trees

Protest Shelter
Tasmania, Australia 2006
Andrew Maynard Architects

Andrew Maynard was getting attention for his innovative designs long before he decided to apply his architectural skills to the protection of the wilderness of his native Tasmania. Now, however, he may just be able to make a name for himself among the great preservationists, as well as among architectural juries. The Styx Valley in southwestern Tasmania is home to the tallest hardwood trees in the world, with an average height of 80 metres, and some rising to 90 metres. As well as being skyscraper in scale, many of the trees are more than 400 years old. As the Styx Valley falls outside the designated World Heritage parkland, logging companies have been allowed to fell the trees, mostly to produce wood chips for export. With the number of trees declining and the lack of any federal protection, activists have taken up positions in the forest, but so far their main habitation, dubbed the 'Global Rescue Station', consists of an open platform supported in the branches of an old gum tree.

Maynard's contribution is a cleverly designed, self-contained unit that combines practicality with unexpected aesthetic and technical achievements. The prototype provides enclosed shelter from the elements, and protects a number of trees with a single habitation.

The two-level capsule accommodation measures a comfortable 3 by 3 metres, with a roof deck, storage and a work area on the lower level, and a sleeping area above. The slender structure (7.9 metres in height) requires minimal roof waterproofing and responds effortlessly to the overwhelming verticality of the surrounding forest. Solar panels on the roof deck supply minimal electric power for lighting and computer operations. Attached to the trees with projecting aluminium pistons, the cabin will remain stable, but, according to Maynard, will also move with the sway of the trees, 'somewhat like a boat in a gently rolling sea'.

Housing a maximum of three people at a time, the shelter attaches to three trees, thereby protecting them from felling. In addition, its span between the trees will prevent the felling of any nearby that might endanger the structure and its inhabitants. Maynard chose to build his protest shelter from farmed timbers, to further the argument for encouraging the use of this type of managed timber supply, as opposed to clearing old-growth forests that are irreplaceable and dwindling. Whether or not one agrees with the tactics, it would be difficult not to be guided by such simple, efficient and beautiful intervention.

crisis containment

Future Shack
Mobile, Australia 2001
Sean Godsell Architects

The humble yet exceedingly robust shipping container has lately been seized upon by architects eager to exploit its easy conversion to modular construction. These industrial-strength prefab components have been used for everything from mountain cabins in California, to hip studio/office pods on the Thames in London. But with his development of the 'Future Shack' concept, Australian architect Sean Godsell has turned the efficiency and economy of the vessels to humanitarian purposes. In his opinion, the need for quick and inexpensive housing in war-torn or refugee-heavy areas, or in regions struck by natural disaster, presents 'an opportunity for architects to provide shelter for fellow human beings in need'.

Mindful of the many difficulties that confront such idealistic endeavours, Godsell has addressed the issues of practicality head-on, firstly by choosing a basic unit that is already widely available. Built to a standard universal size that enables them to be stacked or aligned easily on ship, truck or train, the containers are inherently transportable, as well as flexible in terms of arrangements on the ground. To this ready-made efficiency, Godsell has designed an array of simple elements that help the containers to be erected as housing within twenty-four hours. Brackets and telescoping legs enable the unit to be anchored safely to almost any terrain, while a collapsible parasol roof (packed into the container during transport) provides both shade in hot climates and protection from the rain.

Sufficiently adapted to climate and site, the Future Shacks are each equipped with such necessities as water tanks, solar-power cells, satellite receivers, roof ladders and access ramps. To the bare steel structure has been added thermal insulation and ventilation apertures, and the parasol roof 'can be interchanged with local materials such as thatch, mud and stick, palm leaves, and so on', according to its designer. The modules can be fitted with bathroom/kitchen facilities as required.

When the units are no longer needed, they can be repacked and relocated, or stockpiled for future use. The Future Shack, says Godsell, 'can legitimately be described as a fully recyclable, fully self-sustainable architecture'. It is also not bad to look at, with the simple utilitarian design recalling themes of Modernism – minus the great glazed sections, but elegant nonetheless. So while global response to poverty, disaster and civil war make incremental progress on the agenda of each new political summit, the Future Shack is a great leap toward restoring a modicum of civilization and dignity to those who perhaps need it most.

By adapting a standard cargo container, Godsell hopes to answer at least some of the global need for temporary housing and emergency shelter. The interior is insulated and lined in durable plywood, with basic components added. All necessary parts can be packed and transported within the container.

'The universal nature of the container means that the houses can be stockpiled and easily transported throughout the world.'

a beer in the bush

ZigZag Cabin
Wollombi, New South Wales, Australia 2003
Drew Heath Architects

It was conceived 'as a playful folly from a single beer-coaster sketch', says architect Drew Heath of his compact cabin, which he describes as 'a caravan without wheels'. The shelter for sleeping, sitting and cooking was designed for Sydney-based clients who wanted a rural retreat, but not the sprawling, imposing kind. Here, the architect was aiming for 'a campsite feel', hoping to offer an alternative to larger permanent structures that are appearing in the Australian bush. And with this magic box of a building, in which perspectives, panels and compartments constantly reveal surprising details and vistas, he may yet succeed.

The cabin is made from hardwood framing, timber cladding with a fibre cement sheet, and corrugated metal for the roof. The interior is clad in masonite with a timber floor and plywood joinery. These very basic materials and the simple cubic form are given a dynamic lift with the zig-zag pattern of the window apertures, which not only adds visual interest, but also opens up long and short views into the woods. Opened and closed in a multitude of combinations, the arrangement of windows ensures that the experience inside is never static, and provides a degree of fine-tuning not expected in such pared-down construction. The

controlled lines also break up the building into its component panels of glass, timber and cement.

A range of functions and vistas have been worked into the very compact design. The lower-level windows look out to the land and bush, whereas the vertical windows reveal sectional views of the trees and those at the top look into the tree canopy. There are two sleeping areas, one on the ground floor and another

in a loft, reached by ladder. The living room is an open deck that is only slightly removed from the natural setting.

Not content with the achievement of a highly sufficient unit, Heath used the opportunity to draw attention to his own architectural influences, as well as the inspiration of the bush. With Gerrit Rietveld's 1924 Schröder House in mind, the architect decided to paint the various panels using a colour specifier to match hues from the landscape, so that even with these chromatic touches, the building would sit 'comfortably' with its surroundings. Using a painterly technique of overlaid brush strokes, he was able to build a subtle texture that helps the panels to blend with the rough surfaces of the surrounding trees, rocks and earth. On other sections, the wood is ageing like part of the bush.

'I have always believed that if you looked hard enough, you'll find almost every colour within the landscape.'

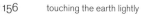

The building expresses many features of the Australian building tradition in its use of wood and corrugated metal sheeting, but also reveals the architect's more Modernist influences. Using a limited range of materials, Heath has created a work that is very fresh and full of surprises.

'The small interior intentionally forces the users out onto the deck and beyond into the Australian bush.'

round and round the garden

Tree Spheres
Vancouver, British Columbia, Canada 2000
Tom Chudleigh

What is it about getting up into the trees? It is a desire that we associate with childhood, and yet in some undeveloped societies it is still the best and safest place to have a home. Potentates of the past used the folly excuse for building little outdoor pleasure palaces, nestled in the branches of a friendly oak or cedar. Now engineer and designer Tom Chudleigh has decided to feed the tree-filled fantasy of otherwise sensible adults by combining the clandestine joys of tree-sitting with the delights of the compact capsule. With a career in boatbuilding behind him, Chudleigh has mastered the smooth joins and curves, as well as the watertight properties of wood, glue and good sealant. His inspiration was the desire to preserve the forest of his native Vancouver Island, an area already badly affected by logging. 'Even when city folk move out to the country,' he explains, 'the first thing they do is clear at least a 30-metre-square piece of land. I wanted to enable people to inhabit the forest without taking it down first.'

The basic structure is a circular frame onto which the wood is laminated, with insulation between the interior and exterior layers. The interior of the first sphere, named Eve, measures 2.8 metres in diameter,

wide enough for two adults and one child to lounge comfortably. Inside, the sphere is equipped with storage and a double bed, sofa and table, along with electricity and phone lines. The eye of the sphere, a circular window measuring a metre across, is like the great oculus of the woods. (Images of some kind of forest-obsessed James Bond villain posting an army of these pods on his heavily guarded private island do come to mind.) This window provides the peephole that makes the tree-sitting experience so fascinating.

Access to the sphere is via more traditional wooden steps that wind around the trunk of a nearby tree and lead to a suspension bridge. The bridge and sphere are held in place by nothing more complicated (or reassuring, perhaps) than good old hemp ropes. So a certain amount of bounce and sway is to be expected. But this is part of the desired experience, and to make this experience more widely available, Chudleigh is working on fibreglass versions of the sphere that can be made more cheaply and, therefore, in quantity. Chudleigh has designs to build a village of his spheres, perhaps a dozen hung together in proximity. Then the James Bond vision really will take hold. But from inside, it's still all about seeing the forest for the trees.

'To live in and among the trees and to use them is my foundation. It depends upon me maintaining a healthy ecosystem. It also gives me back a magic environment right outside my door. Like a bird in a nest.'

Chudleigh uses several vertical lines to distribute the stress on the trees. The sphere is fixed to the centre of a roughly equilateral triangle of three horizontal tethers: the suspension bridge in front and two further ties at the back.

flexing its muscle

'Hybrid Muscle'
Chiang Mai, Thailand 2003
R&Sie(n) with Philippe Parreno

It was a straightforward commission from Rirkrit Tiravanija, who had a piece of land in a field of rice paddies and wanted a work- and exhibition space for visiting artists. He also wanted the building to create its own electricity, to remain off the power grid. Little did he know that he would provide the impetus for a structure that begs the question whether art imitates life, or vice versa. François Roche, of Parisian-based architectural firm R&Sie(n) and film-maker Philippe Parreno now view their collaborative effort as an inseparable work of film and architecture.

The atmosphere of Parreno's film *The Boy from Mars* is surreal science fiction, a largely silent meditation in which the building and its natural context appear to be the main protagonists. The action involves a harnessed water buffalo steadily working an elaborate system of pulleys as the semi-transparent, caterpillar-shaped building glows warmly behind him. Fuzzy figures appear in the film, but their origin and purpose is unclear. The film poses the question of who, or what, is alien, and why? The building, ex-film, is alien to the surroundings, but also well suited in the rice field, its low profile and translucence undulating rhythmically against a line of native trees. Coming here is a little like visiting a film set, except that this particular film set takes itself seriously as architecture, ironically more so than many purpose-built structures. Designed to blend with its surroundings and to generate its own power in the local old-fashioned way, through animal muscle, it is unintrusive and environmentally sensitive, but also sturdy and protective.

Though the marshy ground necessitated the use of concrete for the base, the elongated curve of the roof and walls is clad in lightweight recycled plastic sheets laid over wooden supports. A steel counterweight, weighing 2 metric tonnes, is repeatedly lifted by the animal, generating electricity that is stored in a battery for later use in lighting, computers and cell phones. From a distance, it appears like a barge floating lazily, or, with water buffalo in harness, being pulled slowly over the marshy fields. Parreno and Roche both delight in the blurring of boundaries between art and architecture, real and surreal, and yet, in the cold light of day, the primitive simplicity of the structure and its mechanics works in a very practical fashion.

[previous page] From a distance, the building appears like a barge, floating lazily or being pulled slowly over the marshy fields.

[this page] The interior is not much more than a basic tented shelter. But there is electricity, produced by animal power, that can be used for lighting and computer equipment.

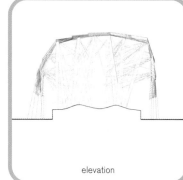

elevation

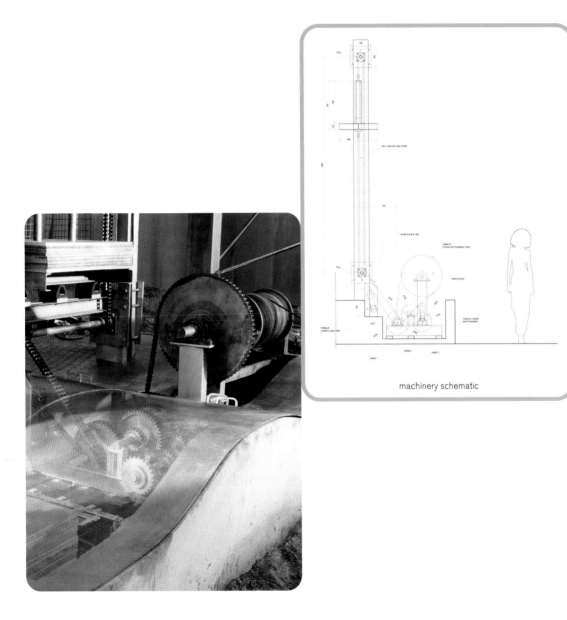

machinery schematic

Having made a name for himself with his space-age, lightweight and transportable structures (see *XS*, volume 1), Richard Horden has guided his students at the Institute of Architecture and Product Design in Munich toward the promise of quality compact living in transportable form. Combining the low-cost and precision design specifications available to a structure made of prefabricated components with the need to conserve precious urban space, Horden and his university teaching assistants, including Lydia Haack of Haack Höpfner, developed the Micro-Compact House, or 'm-ch'. Horden's students in Munich, as well as those at the Tokyo Institute of Technology, developed the concept over four years before launching the prototype in November 2005, as part of a student village commissioned by Studentenwerk München eV (Student Housing Authority). With the aid of telecommunications' and manufacturers' sponsorships, the team created seven of the 2.65-metre cubes, inhabited for the winter semester by six chosen students and Horden himself.

The layout of the beautiful little cube, say the architects, is based on the traditional Japanese tea house. And it is not just the clean white interior that makes this little living closet so much more appealing than your average trailer home at several times the size. Since the permanent division of rooms is impractical in such a small space, the interior functions in a highly logical system of separation and overlap. Technically it is split up into 'zones', with the wet services zone including the toilet, shower and kitchen facilities. But then, of course, dividing lines are blurred. The entrance and kitchen circulation area, which also gives access to seating in the dining space below, are located on a central access. An upper-level sleeping bunk, which can sleep two, folds away during the day, while the sunken dining area can be used as a second double bed. Of course, the latest technology in flat plasma-screen

televisions, microchip circuitry and slimline computers make living small more of a luxury than it was in the age of cabinet-housed home entertainment systems.

Horden's predilection for the lightweight and movable is apparent everywhere. The core structure is made from insulated vacuum aluminium panelling, mounted on timber and galvanized aluminium sections. The houses require no extra furniture and

come with all the energy and communications systems built in, and, being raised off the ground, they have a minimal impact on the environment. Horden claims they are ideal for business travellers, as holiday homes, or for short-term residential or academic use. However, there does seem one rather obvious drawback: the cubes are so mini, so lightweight and so darn irresistible, you could just see home robbery taking on a new meaning.

'A reduction in building volume also reduces man's intrusion in the natural environment and should, therefore, enhance our experience of nature.'

The interiors are thoroughly organized and the functions clearly mapped, though necessarily overlapping. The table folds down to form one bed, while the panel above it forms another, though this can be propped up to increase headroom during the day. The toilet, shower and kitchen line up along one wall to form the compact 'wet zone'.

poetic utility

Small forms that function beautifully

If form married with function always produced bonny offspring, then we would have little reason to remark on a job well done. However, we know from inaccessible phone booths, unpleasant public toilets and inhospitable bus shelters that structures built to function (and sometimes they do not even meet this criteria well) do not always do so in a way that is pleasant to behold. Yet we know how uplifting it can be to experience functional forms that do their job well. How positive it must feel to enter Marlon Blackwell's HoneyHouse, for example, to appreciate the produce of the colony and the practical and graceful form of the building itself, all working in concert to a glorious harmony.

Harmonizing with the environment, too, is a footbridge in the Swiss Alps that helps hikers and walkers navigate the awe-inspiring terrain with little interruption to the natural visual rhythm of the countryside. Construction in aid of human interaction can also be green, even if designed for urban sites. The architect of the HALO phone booth, Lance Hosey, has often addressed the environmental responsibilities of architects both in his designs and through his writing. He is concerned with building in a way that optimizes use and minimizes waste, creating a space that meets our advanced technological needs and embracing that technology to get the most efficiency out of the building process. Chilean architect Felipe Assadi, addressing a different type of wastage, produced a structure for storing fruit that requires no artificial refrigeration, but keeps the produce from spoiling before being transported to local markets.

From the marriage of form and function to marriage in the legal and human sense, the architecture of Klein Dytham in Japan is that of ceremony and celebration. Perhaps functional is not the most romantic description for a wedding chapel, but the design answered a brief to serve a particular purpose, with a simple practical focus, as well as, of course, other less tangible requirements in the areas of romance and beauty. From union to reunion, matrimonial bonds to dissolving political difference – weighty obligations for a slight structure by Brückner & Brückner that attempts to reconcile the formerly divided cultures of Germany and the Czech Republic, separated physically and psychologically during the decades of the Cold War. Can architecture bring unity? It can most surely help, as

Cohen & Judin's comprehensive plan for the disparate elements of the Nelson Mandela Museum makes clear. Through a series of modest pavilions that serve as information points and communal shelters, the architects created a project that includes and promotes community. Of course, buildings that serve the natural environment possess green credentials at the outset. But Matali Crasset's bold and beguiling pigeon loft does so with remarkable aplomb, sensitivity and adherence to the needs of humans and animals alike.

All of the projects in this chapter make prudent use of materials, some emphasizing local resources and practices, like the Mandela pavilions and a very different project that also fosters communal experience, a ferry shelter in Scotland. Employing familiar regional techniques of white-washed masonry and black roofs, the structure is open to the sky, then narrows to a vanishing point that expands again to a wide view over the water. This idea of pointing the viewer's gaze and then opening up the panorama could be said to reflect the aim of the book: to focus on an idea of green building, and then reveal the expansive and truly inspiring range of possibilities.

sweetness and light

HoneyHouse
North Carolina, USA 1998
Marlon Blackwell

They are natural-born builders, with millions of years of construction techniques hard-wired in their genes. They also make honey, and the 70-year-old beekeeper living near the top of Little Terrapin Mountain in North Carolina needed a place to store it all. It was time for architect Marlon Blackwell and his team to revisit a house they had designed in 1990, and figure out a way to combine a honey store, car port and work area in a way that complemented the existing house and the environment. In the forest just beyond the house are four beehives where the locally prized sourwood honey, which the resident sells at markets and along the roadside, is continually produced.

Taking their cue from the bees themselves and from centuries of beekeeping, the architects chose a compartmentalized design that recalls the four-sided hive box. These boxes are successful for both keeper and bee, because 'the moveable frames allow the stored comb honey to be removed without upsetting or destroying the brood chamber.' Blackwell points out that it is the 'efficiency of the beekeeper's equipment, and the bee's willingness to adapt to and use it', that has ensured 'the continual production of honey and the survival of the colony'. This symbiotic relationship was an important theme in the development of the design, so it made sense to integrate the age-old beehive pattern into the structure.

Being elevated from the ground, the steel-and-glass honey wall keeps the refined product safely away from vermin and insects, and, with its rows of window boxes, is a naturally illuminated display case. In the multi-functional structure, this wall forms one side of the enclosed workspace, a box-container-style room that features multiple storage units and a work counter with processing equipment. The inverted metal wing roof, which is a visual counterpoint to the existing house, shelters both the workroom/honey wall and the car-port space next door. Tongue-and-groove pine and weathered metal supports blend with the verdant natural setting. All the steel surfaces were allowed to rust for nine months before being sealed, to produce the desired patina. Combining glass with steel, solidity and transparency, the winning element of this design is the faceted glass wall, where light is filtered and reflected through and around the pots of natural golden delight.

site plan

honeybox diagram

poetic utility

According to the architect, the structure's single most prominent and complex element is the unique steel plate and faceted glass wall that acts to organize the display of honey and to filter natural light. Other elements, wall and roof planes, seem to be set lightly around that organizational centre. The order of the honeybox can be seen in the rationale of the design.

a river runs through it

Footbridge
Boudry, Switzerland 2002
Geninasca Delefortrie

The alps of western Switzerland is an area of startling natural beauty – peaks give way to hidden valleys, rolling hills to dramatic gorges. In 1999, the regional park authority held a competition to build a footbridge over the River Areuse in the area around the little town of Boudry, to accommodate the many hikers and leisurely walkers that come to explore the mountains in all seasons. The winning design by Laurent Geninasca and Bernard Delefortrie makes a safe passage over the fast-flowing river with minimal impact on the site, and still manages to be something of beauty itself.

Traversing a 27-metre gap, the boxed form is made of thin timber slats that run lengthwise, drawing the eye in through the structure, as if through a light-filled tunnel. Undulating slightly, the bridge, strengthened by steel beams and vertical supports, makes a graceful, organic curve across the river. It also arcs gently upward to allow for rising river water. Because the two sides of the gorge differ in character, the bridge form was adapted to fit each location. One end of the bridge has a larger opening made possible by the open, flatter terrain, while the other end, where the bank is steep and craggy, is smaller. Emphasizing this change in aspect, the box grows progressively smaller toward

the steeper bank and the slats converge, creating a vanishing point in the perspective through the structure. From the narrow end, the view is of a great, widening entry to the forest beyond.

Sunlight and breeze flow through the trellis-like sides and roof as through the many trees. Following the curve of shape and shadow, the viewer is reminded of the bend and swirl of the river itself, all of which coincides with the architects' aim of 'listening to place'. Though they were acutely aware of the primacy of the site, Geninasca and Delefortrie feel that their design represents 'not a submission to place, but a respect'. In crossing the footbridge, they hope, one feels protected without being oppressed, 'as if the voyage were through the branches of the trees'. In this they have succeeded. Creating a screen rather than a barrier to the landscape, a passage that, in keeping with the journey, takes in the natural surroundings while moving delicately through them.

The components of pre-treated stained fir were brought to the site by helicopter and assembled in about a week. No two pieces of the structure are identical.

'When a place speaks, the most constructive reaction is to listen, and then to enter into a dialogue with it.'

well-wired

HALO Communications Booth
Prototype, USA 2001
Lance Hosey

'Communication' being the watchword for the millennium, it makes sense that addressing the need for wired, or wireless, centres would be uppermost in designers' minds. Architect Lance Hosey has turned his own mind to a number of projects that have decidedly green properties, from a prefab community garden centre to a mobile classroom to an urban 'eco-toilet'. He has also given thought to wireless centres, in which we want to communicate unplugged but not totally unprotected. His HALO booth veers more toward the high-tech than do many self-proclaimed 'green' projects, but does so using methods that do not mean high wastage. Though it appears like a high-tech fun house, the sort of thing that might accommodate single-occupancy space travel, the compact design is highly functional, efficient and grounded in the need to use materials well.

Hosey, a vocal supporter of ecologically friendly building techniques, highlights the efficiency of the booth's monocoque shell, which 'conserves resources by optimizing the relationship between surface and volume, integrating structure with skin'. Simply put, what envelops the structure is what holds it up. This skin is a 'super-insulated polymer' that prevents heat gain and loss; the interior temperature is regulated using a solar-powered system. Though the prototype has yet to be completed, Hosey is keen to ensure that the components can all be prefabricated, so that mass production can be attained with a minimum of waste and that all the fittings can be manufactured to the same high standard. He also argues that prefabrication means the overall assembly will be tighter, further controlling heat loss/gain in the finished booth.

This is a work of community architecture, to be placed in key pedestrian areas where members of the public can duck in with a laptop, Blackberry or mobile phone for a little privacy and information exchange. The wireless Internet service would be provided for a fee, and the phone user would rediscover that nostalgic experience of making a call in private. Of course, the shape and appearance of the HALO will draw attention to itself both as a piece of public architecture and as something fun to look at. Hosey did not hit on the spiralling ovoid form by accident; he hopes that along with providing a public service, the HALO booth might also become an iconic landmark like the red British phone box, which is coming back by popular demand. In other words – verbal, text or digital – plus ça change.

fruitful thinking

Temporary Fruit Warehouse
Santiago, Chile 2001
Felipe Assadi

It is often the simplest structures that we find most beguiling, usually because there is a hidden complexity or purpose to their accessible form. This 10-metre-long wooden storage facility was designed to answer a basic need, storing fruit between harvest and transport. Of course, there were particular considerations like protecting the fruit from insects, the need for adequate ventilation, and keeping the fruit well spaced so that any rotting specimens would not contaminate a large portion of the harvest. But simplicity was the abiding principle from the beginning, when architect Felipe Assadi chose the standard wooden fruit box as his module and built from there. From this humble starting point, Assadi created a structure that is utterly utilitarian and a delight to behold in the landscape.

The site is a 4.5-hectare parcel outside Santiago belonging to the client, who grows apples, peaches, oranges, pears and cherries, more for a horticultural hobby than for a livelihood. His produce is sold commercially, however, and must be stored on site before being transported by truck to local markets. Logically, Assadi arranged his storage structure into five compartments, one for each type of fruit, so as to keep those of different acidities from contact with each other. Within each compartment the drawers/boxes are set four wide and two deep, with extra space for handling. Stacking the units eight high results in 320 drawers total in a neatly organized, efficient unit. Having sorted out the storage into a tidy geometric puzzle, the architect added fine steel mesh inside the doors to allow ventilation and keep insects away. A zinc roof keeps the rain off and reflects sunlight.

The appeal of the building lies in the subtle details and concealed functions of its minimal design. Hardy materials and a basic form are made more intriguing by the irregular ventilation openings, which create a pattern across the wood cladding that brings to mind digital imagery, or some sort of high-tech sensors. While there is something satisfying in its low-tech construction – framed in steel and engineered composite wood, filled with wood crates and clad in local hardwood – there is also a dignified approach that lifts the structure into the realm of art.

The structure is meant to be seen as a whole box, so the framing was well hidden beneath the ordered cladding. At the same time, the architect says the façade itself was made to look like stacks of fruit boxes, with some boxes missing.

Built on a module determined by the size of a standard wooden fruit box, the structure is a highly rational and yet incredibly appealing object. Open panels provide ventilation, while a zinc roof keeps the store watertight.

Wedding chapels have long held a reputation for fussiness and kitsch. But although this is a purpose-built model set in the grounds of a resort hotel, taste, glamour, and yes, romance, have made their way into the delicate design by architects Astrid Klein and Mark Dytham. The chapel holds a mere eighty guests, so its intentions were always intimate. Set in a small pond, it appears to float like a giant flower on the water, completely separate from the more mundane architecture of the hotel itself.

The chapel design was inspired by local flora, in particular the small, yellow Rempukusou flower. The shape of the building suggests 'two leaves that have seemingly fluttered to the ground'. Essentially a spherical section, the structure is made up of a fixed glass form (one leaf), and a metal shutter that is the second, moveable leaf and akin to a shuttered eye. The shutter has been perforated with 4,700 holes that depict a swirling floral motif. Fitted with acrylic 'lenses', the perforations allow natural light to project a delicate lacy pattern onto the white fabric inside the chapel during the day. At night the chapel glows, with the floral design and glazed section illuminated from within. The wedding ceremony can be enhanced with a dramatic effect by the mechanics of the 11-ton door, designed to lift 'like a bride's veil' at the end ceremony, presenting the pond around the the little park beyond to the newly married vice versa. After the ceremony has ended ar cylinder has been opened, the wedding par pond on carefully aligned stepping stones t the lawn where the celebrations begin.

To highlight the dramatic contrast between dark and light, as well as the 'white purity' of the moment (and perhaps the bride), the architects maintained a dark interior, using blackened timber on the walls and a floor laid in black granite. Black timber benches have back rests made of cast acrylic, with a light-green flower design set into the 20-millimetre thickness to produce a watery effect. With the shutter down, the pattern on the benches is meant to recall a field of flowers that seems to sway in front of the white backdrop.

While references to veils and purity suggest a cloying sentimentality, the building itself is far more subtle and sophisticated. And though thoroughly modern in style and materials, the wedding chapel exudes all the grace and refinement of a Japanese ceremony, but with a touch of romance.

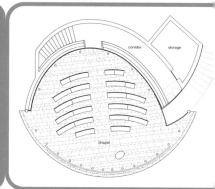

The white steel 'leaf' structure is perforated with 4,700 holes in a floral pattern. Each hole has an acrylic lens, so that the whole piece emulates a pergola, while also referring to a bridal veil. The steel framework of the inner glass panel recalls the veins of a leaf.

The 11-ton door, the 'veil', lifts silently at the end of the ceremony, 'almost like a sheet of fabric', in thirty-eight seconds.

dissolving the iron curtain

Meeting Place
German–Czech Border 2003
Brückner & Brückner Architekten

At the place where the geographic boundaries of Germany and the Czech Republic meet, there are rolling hills – green and carpeted with wildflowers in summer, thick with untouched snow in winter. Like many political borders, it seems an arbitrary line that is imposed on the landscape. But history tells us that this line was not always so arbitrary, and was a very real impediment during the decades of World War II and the Cold War. Now, with no fences or barriers visible, it is difficult to imagine that harsh reality. As the architects of this little room of reconciliation have put it: 'Ideologies have disappeared in society, as well as in architecture, on both sides of the border. The concept of the enemy has vanished, leaving an empty space.'

Into that space, architects Peter Brückner and Christian Brückner have set a modest but profound structure that, rather than serving as a memorial, acknowledges the divide of the past while demonstrating a unified present. A conscious choice of local materials from both countries – Bohemian larchwood, Palatine granite – is framed by steel and illuminated by glass. The confrontation of political ideologies is represented by the contrasting two sides of the building. Oriented northward, it presents a wooded side to the East and its granite face to the West. In the central chamber, the two sides meet – granite and wood face each other, and a block stone table with seats on either side invites visitors to do the same. An inscription in both Czech and German draws the observer in to become a participant.

Reconciliation through confrontation seems to be the modus operandi, highlighting past division so that it can be overcome. But there is also an overwhelming

sense of unity. Each strip of wood and granite, has been cut to the same dimensions (3 metres by 15 centimetres by 5 centimetres), and equal-sized sections of each are interspersed with narrow bands of glazing that become wider as the wall grows higher, a gesture that implies dissolving these man-made boundaries altogether. In the ceiling the two materials, wood and stone, come together to form a solid joint that deliberately casts a shadow into the room, an effect that 'recalls the shadow that the past and half a century of separation have thrown onto the land'. As the open landscape is allowed to dominate the little shelter, and sunlight to permeate its walls, there is at least the suggestion that the natural topography is greater than the restrictions we force upon it.

Glazed gaps between the solid block and wood walls become larger toward the top, helping the building to 'dissolve'. The rough, angular exterior is meant to contrast with the smooth interior.

'The screw joints remain visible on the outer sides,
taking up the inhuman character of the Iron Curtain.'

lofty ambitions

Pigeon Loft
Cambrai, France 2004
Matali Crasset with André Morin

The capsule form is a reference to the clay huts that the ancient Egyptians used to house the pigeons they kept for food and for relaying messages. The bright colour and details highlight the enthusiasm of contemporary pigeon fanciers in this region of northwest France. Set within the 30-acre sports-and-recreation park of Val du Riot, the Pigeon Loft came about as the result of a proposal from the head of the local pigeon society, which won the support of the tourist board and Artconnexion, a community organization that aims to bring contemporary art projects to public spaces. Designer Matali Crasset's bold ideas won over pigeon enthusiasts and park directors alike, being a far cry from the 'rough wooden huts' they were used to seeing.

Crasset was pleased to do something that was 'a living, working place, not just a pretty shell'. Though the shell she created is pretty enough, the interior does function as a working pigeon house. It is also an educational space. Interspersed with the sections of perches and mesh are diagrams of the structure, with notes detailing the uses of the building, the needs and lifestyle of the birds, and the world of pigeon-fancying. Visiting schoolchildren are provided with 'toolkit' aprons to help them in their learning.

The design is striking not just in its bright colour and outward appearance, but also in its elegantly simple plan. The interior framework, constructed by a local specialist in wooden artworks, is made from moisture-resistant, laminated wood, shaped into numerous curved supports and crossbeams. A steel mast in the centre provides structural support. The dome is covered in polyester resin and includes an elevated top section that allows for ventilation. These details were developed in consultation with pigeon fanciers, who advised on such things as keeping the interior free from damp and the correct size of the openings for the birds. A bright red cube hanging out like a postbox is the 'sick room', where unwell or new birds are kept to recuperate and habituate themselves to their new home.

Clearly visible from across the park, the pigeon loft is a tribute to the local bird population, and more. As the director of the public arts programme that made the structure possible describes it: 'This loft is simultaneously a work of art, a place of popular tradition, and an educational tool for the general public.'

A framework of curving vertical members and cross-supports, prefabricated from moisture-resistant laminated wood, attaches to a central steel mast and creates areas that can be easily partitioned into separate internal spaces. The bright colour is a beacon to both birds and humans.

point of departure

Ferry Shelter
Tiree, Scotland 2003
Sutherland Hussey Architects

Light and dark, open and closed, solid and transparent – it is a modern intervention on a rugged landscape that weaves contrasts into a unified experience. The compact and elegant ferry shelter is the result of an initiative by the Scottish Arts Council to create a structure for the small island of Tiree, off the west coast of Scotland. The project was meant to be a collaboration between disciplines, for which architects Charlie Sutherland and Charlie Hussey, artists Jake Harvey, Donald Urquhart, Glen Onwin and Sandra Kennedy, and engineer David Narro joined efforts. The result is a sculptural enclosure that provides protection from the natural elements, but also celebrates them.

The building is composed of three parts that follow on from one another and comprise a physical and mental journey, for which the building was dubbed 'An Turas'. The first component is the roofless white-walled corridor, which leads from the ferry waiting area toward a framed view of the bay at the end of the piece. The walls rise up 2.6 metres on either side, intentionally drawing the gaze up to the clear sky above. Walking thus, sheltered from the bracing wind, the viewer then enters the covered bridge, which straddles an old stone dike, going from bright light to darkened space, from

exposure to protected enclosure. Yet the timber bridge structure has open slats at the bottom perimeter of the walls, so that both the stone dike and the wild growth are visible below. The enclosure doesn't become total until you reach the glass box at the end, where the view is then all-encompassing.

Using stark white for the corridor walls and black felt over timber for the bridge, the design pays homage to the traditional black-and-white buildings of the island, which consist of squat white-painted stone walls and dark thatch, or more recently felt, roofs. The bridge construction is also meant to refer to traditional timber work, as well as to the boat-building industry of the island. The end chamber, with its glass walls and roof, then almost projects the viewer into the scene beyond, so that from the sky above the corridor to the ground visible beneath the bridge, to the glass-framed view, the natural environment is ever present, however mediated by the structure. The glass roof collects rainwater, which makes lapping shadows as the wind blows. Conceived as 'a linear cut in the landscape', An Turas proceeds from inward to outward, revealing glorious moments of its setting, even while offering respite from it.

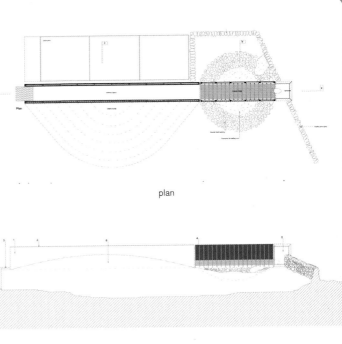

plan

elevation

The white-walled corridor, black bridge and glassed-in belvedere create a progression of experiences while leading the visitor toward the sea. They also present a quick lesson in the natural resources of the region and traditional building techniques.

'It is hoped that the shelter will reflect some of the qualities of the island – the big sky, the white beaches, the black houses dotted over the land – all distilled as a line in the landscape.'

Ferry Shelter

community building

Nelson Mandela Museum Pavilions
Eastern Cape, South Africa 2001
Cohen & Judin Architects

When the South African Department of Arts, Culture, Science and Technology (DACST) decided to erect a museum dedicated to the life and work of former president Nelson Mandela, the project became one of communal, as well as cultural, benefit. In consultation with the local development forum, architects Nina Cohen and Hilton Judin developed a plan that they say changed the concept of museum-as-storage for dormant objects from the past, to one that actively serves the present needs of the wider community. To do this, they linked museum centres at three separate sites through a series of pavilions, 'drop-off points' that would point routes to the nearby villages and to the new cultural spaces. This method would not only tie the outlying villages to one another, and everyone to the new museum facilities, it would also provide much-needed practical amenities for the widely dispersed population.

The pavilions work as shaded meeting points, information kiosks and, perhaps most importantly, sheltered water sources. In an area where women and children still make long journeys to fill water containers from rivers and distant solar-powered bore holes, the provision of a protected, welcoming source for drinking water and washing becomes a shared resource, strengthening ties between villages into a single community. The three sites of this unconventional museum agglomeration comprise a former municipal building in Umtata, a temporary exhibition and meeting space in Qunu, where Mandela spent his childhood, and the remains of the family homestead at Mvezo, Mandela's birthplace. Though the latter village was forcibly removed by the apartheid government in the 1960s, some remains are extant, and the new structure serves as both an information and contemplation space, as well as part of the preservation of the historic site.

The Mvezo pavilion, which will be joined by a communal washing and fresh-water facility, is perhaps most representative of the spirit and focus of the project. Using local skills and materials, the building is a modest but eloquent tribute to the man and his

struggle, and to the integrity of the natural surroundings. Stone and unfinished woven branches, log poles and plank-wood flooring tie the structure very much to the local building tradition.

The projects were designed to employ a large percentage of contractors and suppliers deemed disadvantaged, thereby bolstering the local economies. As the structures are completed and draw tourism to the region, more permanent jobs will be created. This is a museum project about nurturing the parts to make a united and successful whole, very much in the spirit of its eponymous subject.

[previous page] The pavilion is one of a series that helps point visitors toward the three different sites that make up the Nelson Mandela museum, and provide sheltered areas for washing, collecting water and communal gathering.

[this page] Basic forms and local materials enhance the user-friendly character of the pavilions.

wash-trough section

plan

front section

sources

Project Credits
Architect Information
Picture Credits

project credits

Sitooterie [36]
Client: Barnard's Farm, Essex
Cost: £400,000
Size: 2.4m²
Architects: Thomas Heatherwick Studio

Split/View [38]
Client: Philbrook Museum of Art
Size: 2.4m (width), 9.75m (length)
Architects: Mitnick Roddier Hicks
Project team: Keith Mitnick, Mireille Roddier, Stewart Hicks

Camera Obscura [20]
Client: Village of Greenport, New York
Cost: $170,000
Size: 32.5m²
Architects: SHoP Architects
Project team: Christopher R. Sharples, William W. Sharples, Coren D. Sharples, Kimberly J. Holden, Gregg A. Pasquarelli, Mark Ours, Reese Campbell, Jason Anderson, Keith Kaseman, Basil Lee

Vines Pavilion [42]
Client: Philbrook Museum of Art
Size: 79m²
Designers: MADE
Project team: Ben Bischoff, Oliver Freundlich, Brian Papa, Mitch Snyder, Nik Malkmus

Garden Hut [26]
Client: Private
Cost: € 14,000
Architects: Eightyseven Architects
Project team: Artur Carulla, Rita Lambert

Camera Obscura [46]
Client: The Aegina Academy
Cost: € 30,000
Size: 40m²
Architect/designer: Franz Berzl, Gustav Deutsch

Mirador [30]
Client: Private
Size: 35m²
Architects: Carolina Contreras, Tomás Cortese

Garden Pavilion [50]
Client: The Artists' Garden Cooperative
Size: 4.1m (height), 3m (width), 4m (length)
Architects/designers: Paul Raff Studio, Sasquatch Designlab

Gazebo Kuusi [54]
Client: Private
Size: 15m²
Architect: Juhani Pallasmaa
Project team: Juhani Pallasmaa, Michael Moser (design assistant), Pauli Wetterstrand, Insinööritoimisto Heiskanen RJ Oy (structural engineering)

Think Tank [58]
Client: Private
Architects: Gumuchdjian Architects
Project team: Philip Gumuchdjian

Na Hale 'Eo Waiawi [66]
Client: Honolulu Contemporary Art Museum
Cost: *c.* $10,000
Size: 9.1m (height), 9.1m (width), 7m (length)
Designer: Patrick Dougherty

Toad Hall
Client: Santa Barbara Botanic Garden
Cost: *c.* $12,000
Size: 9.1m (height), 9.1m (width), 9.1m (length)
Designer: Patrick Dougherty

Miele Space Station [prototype] [72]
Cost: € 25,000
Size: 2.8m (height), 2.4m (width), 4.8m (length)
Architects: 2012 Architecten
Project team: Cesare Peeren, Jan Jongert, Denis Oudendijk, Jan Kourbes, Amanda Wood, Bart Steenweg, Meus Weemhof, Friso Leeflang, Steven Barich, Joris en Wout Rockx, Freya van Dien, Gijs de Groot, Marco Broeders, Roeland Vergouwen

Turf House [76]
Client: Department of Foreign Affairs, Government of Ireland
Cost: *c.* £21,000
Size: 12m²
Architects: de Paor Architects
Project team: Tom de Paor, T. Maher, S. Shortt

Ferry Go Round [82]
Client: CBK Groningen
Cost: € 20,000
Size: 5m (height), 9m (width), 9m (length)
Architect: Lambert Kamps
Project team: Lambert Kamps, Tjeerd Veenhoven

Air Bridge [prototype]
Cost: € 25,000
Size: 3 m (height), 3 m (width), 15 m (length)
Architect: Lambert Kamps

Space Maker [prototype]

Cost: € 30,000
Size: 2.5m (height), 15m (width), 15m (length)
Architect: Lambert Kamps

Big Orbits [88]

Client: Big Orbit Gallery
Cost: $57,000 (including donated materials and labour)
Size: 4.3m (diameter), 10.7m (length), 10.7m x 15.2m (gallery)
Architect/designer: Mehrdad Hadighi, Frank Fantauzzi
Project team: Mehrdad Hadighi, Frank Fantauzzi, Anthony Dong, Noboru Inoue, David Misenheimer, Tim Burke, Nicholas Cameron, Marie Carone, Melissa Delaney, Carrie Galuski, Jessica Jamroz, Karen Li, Ted Lutz, Michael Maggio, Matthew Macuso, Kerron Miller, Chris Paa, Gharat Patel, Dan Puff, Joseph Seene, Mike Singh, Korydon Smith, Queenie Tong, Michael Wnuk, Su Yi, David Zielinski

Primary School Building [92]

Client: Governors of Westborough Primary School
Cost: £177,157
Size: 90m²
Architects: Cottrell & Vermeulen Architecture
Project team: Richard Stuart Cottrell, Brian Vermeulen, Buro Happold (structural engineering), Essex Tube Windings Ltd, Papermarc, Quinton & Kaines, CG Franklin Building Ltd

Singing Ringing Tree [98]

Designers: Tonkin Liu Architects
Project team: Mike Tonkin, Anna Liu

Superadobe Structures [prototype] [100]

Architects: Nader Khalili, California Institute of Earth Art and Architecture

Glass Dome [104]

Client: Institute for Lightweight Structure and Conceptual Design (ILEK), University of Stuttgart
Size: 2.5m (height), 8.5m (diameter)
Designers: Lucio Blandini, Werner Sobek (ILEK, University of Stuttgart)
Project team: Lucio Blandini, Bircan Avci, Bartolomiej Halaczek, Roberta Wagner (construction), F. Lausberger (workshop)

Hairywood [112]

Client: The Architecture Foundation
Cost: £16,000
Size: 6.3m (height)
Architects/designers: 6a Architects, Eley Kishimoto
Project team: Tom Emerson, Stephanie MacDonald, Mark Eley, Wakako Kishimoto

Greening of Detroit Pavilion [116]
Client: Anonymous donor
Cost: $144,000
Size: 267.6m²
Architects: Zago Architecture
Project team: Andrew Zago

Loftcube [prototype]
[120]
Cost: € 109,000 (with bathroom and kitchen) or € 89,000 (without)
Size: 39m²; 2.5m (height)
Architects: Studio Aisslinger
Project team: Werner Aisslinger

Urban Nomad Shelters [prototype]
[124]
Size: 1.4m (height), 1.5m (width), 2.7m (length)
Architects: Electroland
Project team: Cameron McNall, Damon Seeley

Puppet Theatre [126]
Client: Harvard University Art Museums
Cost: $50,000
Size: 39m²
Designers: Michael Meredith, Pierre Huyghe
Project team: Michael Meredith, Pierre Huyghe, Geoff von Oeyen, Chad Burke, Zac Culbreth, Elliot Hodges, Fred Holt, Hilary Sample (consultant)

Dream House [132]
Client: Culture Department, Municipality of Huesca
Cost: € 1,200
Size: 4m (height), 1m (diameter)
Architects: Ex Studio
Project team: Iván Juárez, Patricia Meneses

Rucksack House [prototype] [134]
Client: Made to order
Cost: € 40,000 (prototype) or c. € 27,000 (manufactured as a small series)
Size: 6.25m², 3.6m (height)
Designer: Stefan Eberstadt
Project team: Thomas Beck, AKA Engineers (structural engineering); Alfred Mayerhofer, Georg Dobetsberger, Anlagenbau Schlosserei (construction)

Park Pavilion [138]
Client: Culture Department, Hamburg
Cost: € 33,500
Size: 5.7m²
Architects: And8 Architekten
Project team: Achim Aisslinger, Andreas Bracht, Dan Graham (artist), R. Stupperich (consultants)

La Petite Maison du Weekend [144]
Client: Wexner Center for the Arts
Size: 26m²
Architects: Patkau Architects
Project team: Timothy Newton, John Patkau, Patricia Patkau, Coelling Smith Design (builder)

Protest Shelter [prototype] [148]
Cost: A$120,000
Size: 9m², 7.9m (height)
Architects: Andrew Maynard Architects
Project team: Andrew Maynard

Future Shack [prototype] [150]
Cost: A$40,000
Size: 15m²
Architects: Sean Godsell Architects
Project team: Sean Godsell

ZigZag Cabin [154]
Client: Private
Cost: A$50,000
Size: 2.4m x 3.6m x 3.3m (cabin); 8m x 2m (deck)
Architects: Drew Heath Architects
Project team: Drew Heath

Tree Spheres [prototype] [158]
Cost: wood from C$150,000; fibreglass from C$45,000 (wholesale discounts available)
Size: 2.8m (diameter)
Designer: Tom Chudleigh

'Hybrid Muscle' [162]
Client: The Land, Rirkirt Tiravanija
Cost: $65,000
Size: 130m²
Designers: R&Sie(n), Philippe Parreno
Project team: François Roche, Philippe Parreno, Stéphanie Lavaux, Jean Navarro

Micro-Compact Home [166]
Client: Student Housing Authority, Munich
Cost: c. € 50,000
Size: 2.65m²
Architects: Horden Cherry Lee Architects, Haack Höpfner Architekten
Project team: Richard Horden, Lydia Haack, John Höpfner, Tanja Dietsch, Stephan Koch
Sponsor: O2 (Germany)
Additional sponsorship: Fujitsu Siemens Computers (screens), Siemens–Electrogeräte (kitchen equipment), Vaku–Isotherm (roof insulation panels)

HoneyHouse [174]
Client: Private
Cost: $40,000
Size: 17.8m²; 26.75m² (carport)
Architect: Marlon Blackwell
Project team: Marlon Blackwell, Ati Blackwell, Dianne Meek, Phil Hatfield

Footbridge [178]
Client: Départment de la gestion du territoire, canton de Neuchâtel
Cost: € 150,000
Size: 27.5m (length)
Architects: Geninasca Delefortrie
Project team: Laurent Geninasca, Bernard Delefortrie; C. Perla, Chablais et Poffet (engineering); Technique Metal Sarl (metal structure)

HALO Communications Booth [prototype] [184]
Cost: *c.* $150,000
Size: 3.7m²
Architect: Lance Hosey

Temporary Fruit Warehouse [186]
Client: Private
Size: 15m², 10m (length)
Architect: Felipe Assadi
Project team: Felipe Assadi, Germán Lamarca

Wedding Chapel [190]
Client: Risonare (Hoshino Resort)
Size: 167.9m²
Architects: Klein Dytham Architects
Project team: Astrid Klein, Mark Dytham, Yoshinori Nishimura, Yukinari Hisayama

Meeting Place [194]
Cost: € 10,000
Size: 9m x 1.5m
Architects: Brückner & Brückner Architekten
Project team: Peter Brückner, Christian Brückner

Pigeon Loft [198]
Client: Les nouveaux commanditaires, fondation de France
Cost: € 79,000
Size: 6.2m (height), 5m (depth)
Designers: Matali Crasset Productions, André Morin
Project team: Matali Crasset, André Morin

Ferry Shelter [202]
Client: Tiree Arts Enterprise
Size: *c.* 95m²
Architects: Sutherland Hussey Architects
Project team: Charlie Sutherland, Charlie Hussey; Jake Harvey, Donald Urquhart, Glen Onwin, Sandra Kennedy (artists); David Narro (structural engineer)

Nelson Mandela Museum Pavilions [208]
Architects: Cohen & Judin Architects
Project team: Nina Cohen, Hilton Judin

architect information

6a Architects [112]
6a Orde Hall Street
London WC1N 3JW
UK
tel: +44 20 7242 5422
fax: +44 20 7242 3646
post@6a.co.uk
www.6a.co.uk

2012 Architecten [72]
Gerard Scholtenstraat 100
3035 SR Rotterdam
The Netherlands
tel/fax: +31 10 467 1676
info@2012architecten.nl
www.2012architecten.nl

And8 Architekten [138]
Margaretenstraße 15
20357 Hamburg
Germany
tel: +49 40 430 8811
fax: +49 40 430 8887
office@and8.de
www.and8.de

Felipe Assadi [186]
Malaga 940, Las Condes
Santiago
Chile
tel: +56 2 263 5738
fax: +56 2 207 6984
info@assadi.cl
www.felipeassadi.com

Franz Berzl [46]
Schottenfeldgasse 78/3/7
1070 Vienna
Austria
tel: +43 1 526 72 81
fax: +43 1 523 80 68
franz-berzl@chello.at

Marlon Blackwell [174]
100 West Center Street, Suite 001
Fayetteville, Arkansas 72701
USA
tel: +1 479 973 9121
info@marlonblackwell.com
www.marlonblackwell.com

Lucio Blandini [104]
Institut für Leichtbau Entwerfen
und Konstruieren (ILEK)
University of Stuttgart
Pfaffenwaldring 7
70569 Stuttgart
Germany
tel: +49 711 685 6 62 27
www.uni-stuttgart.de/ilek

Brückner & Brückner Architekten
[194]
Franz-Böhm-Gasse 2
95643 Tirschenreuth, Bavaria
Germany
tel: +49 9631 70150
wue@architektenbrueckner.de

Tom Chudleigh [158]
Box 645
Errington, British Columbia
V0R 1V0
Canada
tel: +1 250 752 9250
tom@freespiritspheres.com
www.freespiritspheres.com

Carolina Contreras,
Tomás Cortese [30]
Las Achiras 3061, dept. 31
Providencia, Santiago
Chile
tel: +56 2 686 56 71
carolina.con@gmail.com
tcortese@gmail.com

Cohen & Judin Architects [208]
17 Commercial Street
Cape Town 8001
South Africa
tel: +27 21 45 1853

Cottrell & Vermeulen
Architecture [92]
1b Iliffe Street
London SE17 3LJ
UK
tel: +44 20 7708 2567
fax: +44 20 7252 4742
info@cv-arch.co.uk
www.cv-arch.co.uk

Matali Crasset Productions [198]
26, rue du Buisson Saint Louis
75010 Paris
France
tel: +33 1 42 40 99 89
matali.crasset@wanadoo.fr
www.matalicrasset.com

Patrick Dougherty [66]
stickwork@earthlink.net
www.stickwork.net

Stefan Eberstadt [134]
Akademie der bildenden Künste
Akademiestraße 2
80799 Munich
Germany
tel: +49 89 167 098
stefan.eberstadt@adbk.mhn.de

Eightyseven Architects [26]
72 Belsize Park Gardens
London NW3 4NG
UK
contact@eightyseven.net
www.eightyseven.net

Electroland [124]
Los Angeles, California
USA
tel: +1 310 915 7650
fax: +1 310 915 7654
contact@electroland.net
www.electroland.net

Eley Kishimoto [112]
[shop] 40 Snowsfields, Southwark
London SE1 3SU
UK
tel: +44 20 7357 0037
www.eleykishimoto.com

Ex Studio [132]
Carrer del Rec 16
Ático 08003 Barcelona
Spain
tel: +34 93 319 7146
exstudio@ex-studio.net
www.ex-studio.net

Frank Fantauzzi [88]
University of Buffalo
Department of Architecture
112 Hayes Hall
3435 Main Street
Buffalo, New York 14214-3087
USA
tel: +1 716 829 3485
faf1@ap.buffalo.edu
www.icebergproject.org

Geninasca Delefortrie [178]
Place-d'Armes 3
CH-2001 Neuchâtel
Switzerland
tel: +41 32 729 99 60
fax: +41 32 729 99 69
gd@gd-archi.ch
www.gd-archi.ch

Sean Godsell Architects [150]
Level 1, 45 Flinders Lane
Melbourne, Victoria 3000
Australia
tel: +61 3 9654 2677
fax: +61 3 9654 3877
godsell@netspace.net.au
www.seangodsell.com

Gumuchdjian Architects [58]
17 Rosebery Avenue
London EC1R 4SP
UK
tel: +44 20 7837 1800
fax: +44 20 7837 3600
philip@gumuchdjian.com
www.gumuchdjian.com

Haack Höpfner Architekten [166]
Agnes-Bernauer-Straße 113
80687 Munich
Germany
tel: +49 89 1239 1731
info@haackhoepfner.com
www.haackhoepfner.com

Mehrdad Hadighi [88]
University of Buffalo
Department of Architecture
112 Hayes Hall
3435 Main Street
Buffalo, New York 14214-3087
USA
tel: +1 716 829 3485
hadighi@ap.buffalo.edu

Drew Heath Architects [154]
www.drewheath.com

Thomas Heatherwick Studio [36]
16 Acton Street
London WC1X 9NG
UK
tel: +44 20 7833 8800
fax: +44 20 7833 8400
studio@thomasheatherwick.com
www.thomasheatherwick.com

Horden Cherry Lee Architects [166]
34 Bruton Place
London W1J 6NR
UK
tel: +44 20 7495 4119
info@hcla.co.uk
www.hcla.co.uk

Lance Hosey [184]
700 East Jefferson Street
Charlottesville, Virginia 22902
USA
tel: +1 434 979 1111
fax: +1 434 979 1112
media@mcdonough.com
www.mcdonoughpartners.com

Lambert Kamps [82]
info@lambertkamps.com
www.lambertkamps.com

Nader Khalili [100]
California Institute of Earth Art
and Architecture
10376 Shangri La Avenue
Hesperia, California 92345
USA
tel: +1 760 244 0614
fax: +1 760 244 2201
calearth@aol.com
www.calearth.org

Klein Dytham Architects [190]
AD Bldg 2F
1-15-7 Hiroo
Shibuya-ku
Tokyo 150 – 0012
Japan
kda@klein-dytham.com
www.klein-dytham.com

MADE [42]
141 Beard Street, Building 12B
Brooklyn, New York 11231
USA
tel: +1 718 834 0171
fax: +1 718 834 0173
info@made-nyc.com
www.made-nyc.com

Andrew Maynard Architects [148]
250 Rae Street
Fitzroy North, Victoria 3068
Australia
tel/fax: +61 3 9486 1123
info@andrewmaynard.com.au
www.andrewmaynard.com.au

Michael Meredith [126]
Department of Architecture
Harvard University Graduate
School of Design
48 Quincy Street
Cambridge, Massachusetts 02138
USA
mmeredith@gsd.harvard.edu
www.gsd.harvard.edu

Mitnick Roddier Hicks [38]
Ann Arbor, Michigan
USA
tel: +1 734 709 2637
info@mitnickroddierhicks.com
www.mitnickroddierhicks.com

Juhani Pallasmaa [54]
Tehtaankatu 13 b 28
00140 Helsinki
Finland
tel: +358 9 669 740
pallasm@clinet.fi

de Paor Architects [76]
12 Mountjoy Parade
Dublin, Ireland
office@depaor.com
www.depaor.com

Philippe Parreno [162]
32, rue Louise Weiss
75013 Paris
France
tel: +33 1 44 23 02 77

Patkau Architects [144]
1564 West 6th Avenue
Vancouver, British Columbia
V6J 1R2
Canada
tel: +1 604 683 7633
info@patkau.ca
www.patkau.ca

Paul Raff Studio [50]
204 Spadina Avenue
Toronto, Ontario M5T 2C2
Canada
tel: +1 416 707 7800
fax: +1 416 352 5954
studio@paulraffstudio.com
www.paulraffstudio.com

R&Sie(n) [162]
24, rue des Maronites
75020 Paris
France
tel: +33 1 42 06 06 69
fax: +33 1 42 08 27 86
rochedsvsie@wanadoo.fr
www.new-territories.com

Sasquatch Designlab [50]
25 Liberty Street, Unit 303
Toronto, Ontario M6K 1A6
Canada
tel: +1 416 530 7773
designlab@ssqtch.ca
www.ssqtch.ca

SHoP Architects [20]
11 Park Place, Penthouse
New York, New York 10007
USA
tel: +1 212 889 9005
fax: +1 212 889 3686
studio@shoparc.com
www.shoparc.com

Werner Sobek [104]
Institut für Leichtbau Entwerfen
und Konstruieren (ILEK)
University of Stuttgart
Pfaffenwaldring 7 und 14
70569 Stuttgart
Germany
tel: +49 711 685 6 62 26
werner.sobek@ilek.uni-stuttgart.de
www.uni-stuttgart.de/ilek

Studio Aisslinger [120]
Oranien Platz, 4
10999 Berlin
Germany
tel: +49 30 315 05400
fax: +49 30 315 05401
studio@aisslinger.de
www.aisslinger.de

Sutherland Hussey Architects [202]
122 Giles Street
Edinburgh EH6 6BZ
UK
tel: +44 131 553 4321
architecture@sutherlandhussey.co.uk
www.sutherlandhussey.co.uk

Tonkin Liu Architects [96]
24 Rosebery Avenue
London EC1R 4SX
UK
tel: +44 20 7837 6255
fax: +44 20 7837 6277
mail@tonkinliu.co.uk
www.tonkinliu.co.uk

Zago Architecture [116]
4600 Woodward Avenue, Suite 311
Detroit, Michigan 48201
USA
tel: +1 313 961 2781
41 East 11th Street, 3rd floor
New York, New York 10003
USA
mail@zagoarchitecture.com
www.zagoarchitecture.com

picture credits